Pullman Trains
In Britain

by
R.W. Kidner

THE OAKWOOD PRESS

This book contains material originally published in *Pullman Cars of the 'Southern'* *1875-1972* (LP164 - published 1987), which it replaces.

British Library Cataloguing in Publication Data
A Record for this book is available from the British Library
ISBN 0 85361 531 4

Typeset by Oakwood Graphics.
Repro by Ford Graphics, Ringwood, Hants.
Printed by The Witney Press, Witney, Oxon.

The 'Brighton Pullman Limited' about 1903, comprising two sets with pup generating vans, and running via the 'Quarry line', hauled by a 'B4' class 4-4-0.
Tucks Famous Expresses No. 11

Front cover: 'Merchant Navy' class Pacific No. 21C11 *General Steam Navigation* with the 'Devon Belle' at Clapham Junction in August 1947. *Rear cover, top*: 'A1' class Pacific No. 60134 *Foxhunter* on the down 'Yorkshire Pullman' near Markham tunnel in June 1960. *Rear cover, bottom*: A Blue Pullman is seen at Paddington in 1960. *(All) Colour-Rail*

Published by
The Oakwood Press (Usk)
P.O. Box 13, Usk, Mon., NP5 1YS.

Contents

The down 'Queen of Scots' near Hatfield on 25th September, 1931, hauled by the booster-fitted 'Atlantic' No. 4419. The first car is the ex-GER one specially rebuilt with large luggage space for this service. *R. Brookman*

Author's Note

There have been Pullmans on British railways for 120 years. There was a shaky period in the 1880s, when the Midland and the Great Northern purchased their cars from the Company, and only the enthusiasm of the London Brighton & South Coast Railway kept them in the public eye; but by 1911 more railways began to use them, and in the 1920s all-Pullman trains gained notable successes. After World War II a number of new Pullman trains were introduced, still using stock of traditional design and livery. From 1960 the cars themselves, which had formerly stood out proudly in a train, became very similar to ordinary coaches, and finally in the 1980s the name Pullman was sometimes used just to denote a superior first class.

Fortunately a number of 'traditional' cars had been purchased privately, and were often seen on the main lines, until restrictions on permissible bogies affected some; but the VSOE still runs and a few are still on private railways. The more modern stock has also largely survived, through several changes in ownership and livery; they may look rather unlike the cars of the Golden Age, but they keep alive the Pullman idea of perfection.

RWK

It was eager with anticipation that the author reserved seats on the first electric 'Southern Belle' to run on 1st January, 1933, and on the evening return train. How would the motored end coaches ride, and how fast - on the down journey many stop watches were seen in action.   *Author*

Chapter One

The Pullman Idea

A stranger seeing a Brighton express at the turn of the century, and noting one or two large American saloons sailing along in the middle of what were mostly six-wheeled carriages, might have wondered what they were doing there. The Pullman car, which ran in its own livery and did not belong to the railway, was certainly an anomaly, though it must be added that at that time most of the goods wagons did not belong to the railways either. It is perhaps surprising that the relationship with the operators, at any rate on the Southern lines, was so harmonious.

George Mortimer Pullman had been building his cars in the USA from the 1860s; they were nothing strange there, being similar to other stock, though offering sleeping and dining facilities. In Britain sleeping cars had been tried, but did not catch on; distances were mostly too short. On the continent of Europe there was more scope, and a company, titled the Compagnie Internationale des Wagons-Lits, had been set up in Belgium in 1872. Pullman also had his eye on that market, and Britain; he first found a partner in the Midland Railway (MR), which was willing to assemble American-made saloons at the Derby works, and to run them in some trains. The first such train ran on 1st June, 1874. They were either sleeping cars or day drawing room cars; diners did not come in until 1879, when Pullman provided one for the Great Northern Railway (GNR). Between 1883 and 1888, as Agreements expired, the MR bought up Pullmans and operated them in its own livery; others were transferred to the London Brighton & South Coast Railway (LBSCR). The few GNR cars were also sold by 1895.

Pullman had certainly forced the railway companies to accept that they must provide dining and sleeping facilities, though this benefited him little and Pullman never again became involved in the UK with sleeping cars. However, the 'Pullman Idea' was not really about eating and sleeping; it was about providing luxury travel above the ordinary first class, and seen to be so by its livery and decor. The company was to provide cars and service of a quality that the railways could not. A few railways accepted this idea, most at that time did not. However, such was the dedication of the management and staff of Pullman that in due course the idea of 'Pullman and Perfection' was created in the public mind, leading to their later adoption on many main lines.

The British Pullman Car Company was formed in 1882, reformed with new management in 1908 and 1915, and then changed little until 1954 when the British Transport Commission started buying up the shares; by January 1963 it was a wholly-owned subsidiary, and later simply part of a Division of British Rail. By that time most of the glamour had gone; there were still privileged rail travellers, but they were mostly businessmen or officials for whom speed meant more than luxury. Real prestige now lay with the private aircraft. The 'Pullman Idea' dwindled; however comfortable a carriage, if station premises are dirty and staff surly, the contentment of Pullman travel cannot be there. Yet the

The Maximum of Luxury
at the Minimum of Cost.

"PULLMAN" and "PERFECTION"

Are synonyms when they refer to Car Building, in which art the Pullman Company leads the world. In elaborate design, substantial construction and luxurious finish, Pullman Cars represent the highest standard of excellence.

Ingenuity and skill are constantly being applied to the improvement of details with a view to adding to the comfort of travel. Every Car is in charge of an experienced, well-trained Conductor, whose services are always at hand from start to finish of a journey, and invalids and ladies with children can always rely upon ready attention to their comfort and convenience.

Cleanliness is also a special feature, coupled with perfect ventilation and good lighting, thus making travelling a real luxury.

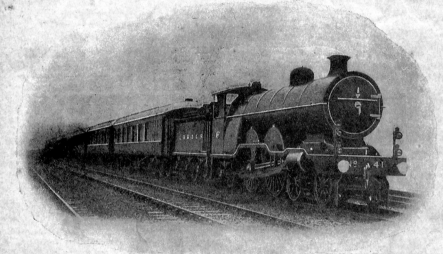

THE SOUTHERN BELLE.

THE MOST LUXURIOUS TRAIN IN THE WORLD. RUNS TWICE DAILY BETWEEN LONDON AND BRIGHTON IN **60** MINUTES.

The PULLMAN COMPANY, Ltd.

Chief London Office—

Victoria Station (S. E. & C. R.), Pimlico, S.W.

Telegraphic Address—"PULLMAN, LONDON."   Telephone No. 4584 VICTORIA.
Thomas Powell, Secretary and Manager.

magic of the name did not die; it was kept going by the preserved Pullman trains described later.

Pullman cars were as stated first assembled at a works set up by the Midland Railway at Derby; after 1888 and until a facility was set up at the former London Chatham & Dover Railway (LCDR) works at Longhedge, assembly was carried out by the LBSCR at Brighton. However, from 1908 most cars were built by UK carriage building firms, Metropolitan, Birmingham, Cravens and Clayton. In 1928 rebuilding work was transferred from Longhedge to a large depot at Preston Park near Brighton.

Because they were built in small batches and for differing purposes, there was in the early days little standardisation. There were also frequent rebuildings and conversions as between parlour, kitchen and brake cars. However, some generalisations are possible: from 1874 to 1895 cars were entirely of wood and ran on four-wheeled bogies of American pattern, roofs being of the clerestory type sloping down at the ends; from 1899 to 1906 they were similar but ran on six-wheeled bogies. From 1908, when cars began to be built in the UK, they ceased to have clerestory roofs; from 1910 to 1914 they were mixed eight-wheeled and twelve-wheeled and had steel frames. No twelve-wheelers were built after 1923; from 1928 steel bodies were used.

The 1932 cars for electric sets were little changed in appearance though with a new design of bogie. Now for 19 years the Slump, the War, and post-War shortages meant that no new Pullmans were built. When some did appear in 1951 the only noticeable change was the use of square lavatory windows in place of the oval ones which had been a feature since 1906. These were the last 'traditional' cars built; in 1960 some new Pullmans were built for the ER East Coast services, but BR Mk I body shells were used.

There were seven main types of car arrangement: parlour cars with seating only, all-first class until 1915; kitchen cars with either 1st or 3rd class seating; bar cars classed or unclassed; composite cars with both 1st and 3rd class seating; brake cars with about one-third given over to luggage space; guard cars with only a seat in one end vestibule; and observation cars of which there were only three, one in Scotland and two on the SR.

The relative requirements of these types of cars varied as contracts or services changed. Some rebuildings were so drastic that one could only take the company's word that it was the same car. In a few cases alterations were to improve exterior styling, as when *Albert Edward* had 16 small windows altered to eight large ones. The largest number of rebuildings were to provide 'end cars'. Although the 1881 'Brighton Limited' had a baggage car, this idea was not continued, as it was expected that most Pullmans would work within trains; it was when all-Pullman trains became popular that end-cars with room for guard and luggage were called for. This did not apply to the 'White Pullman' on the former South Eastern & Chatham Railway (SECR) in 1924, where most of the baggage was sent in custom-sealed boxes on flat wagons, or with the following train, and for this 'guard' cars were created, difficult to recognise as they only differed from parlour cars in having the word 'guard' on one end door.

Dimensions

A casual scanning of published dimensions of Pullman cars can be very confusing, because it is seldom made clear whether the figure refers to 'over body corners', 'over vestibules' or 'over buffers'. In the early days of open platforms, it was natural to measure between the corner posts of the main body, as this was the useful part for accommodation. However, the platforms added some 6 feet, and buffers another 2-2½ feet, so that a '51 ft car' would be about 59½ ft over buffers. The early cars do not seem to have had a standard length; *Alexandra* was 54 ft 'over sills' and 61 ft 0¾ in. over buffers. *Albert Edward* of the same year was 52 ft over sills and 59 ft 0¾ in. over buffers. *The Arundel*, an American-built twelve-wheeler of 1899, was 57 ft 'over corners', 64 ft over vestibules and 65 ft 8 in. overall. The interior dimensions were made up of a 5 ft anteroom with ladies' WC, 31 ft 2 in. main saloon, 5 ft 6 in. anteroom with gents' WC and buffet, 6 ft 6 in. coupé, and 8 ft 6 in. small saloon. The insides of later cars were less complex. An article in the *Locomotive Magazine* stated that Pullmans were 58 ft up to 1894, then 61 ft to 1899, and 64 ft after that; these seem to be approximate lengths over vestibules. The height of the early clerestory-roofed cars was 13 ft. Bogie wheelbases were 8 ft until 1951 (12 ft for 6-wheel bogies) and 8 ft 6 in. after, but there were exceptions: the converted London & North Western Railway (LNWR) cars of 1921 had 9 ft bogies and the London & North Eastern Railway (LNER) all-steel 1928 stock, 10 ft bogies.

Some comparative figures for main dimensions:

	Length over corners	Length over buffers	Height	Width	Weight
	ft in.	ft in.	ft in.	ft in.	Tons
Maud 1877	52 0	59 5	13 2	8 11	27
1906 12-wheel	57 0	65 9	13 0	8 8 ¾	35
'Southern Belle' 1908	57 0	65 4	13 6	8 8 ¾	40
SECR 1910-14	51 0	60 0	12 6 ¾	8 7	31-34
GER 1920 12w.	- -	66 11 ½	12 6	8 10	43
Ex-LNWR 1921	56 9	61 0	12 6 ½	8 7	32
Hastings cars 1926	- -	- -	12 6	8 1	38
All-steel 1928	- -	65 10	12 5	8 7	37-4
6 PUL elec. 1932	59 2 ½	68 8 ¾	12 5	8 11 ½	43
'Golden Arrow' 1951	- -	65 10	12 5	8 5 ½	40-41

The weights of the 'Southern Belle' cars were: motor brakes 62 tons, 1st buffets 43 tons, 3rd parlours 40 tons. The overall length of the set was given officially as 335 ft. However, this assumes the buffers in a considerable state of compression, as the trailer cars had a length between vestibule plates of 66 ft and the motor cars were 66 ft 8¾ in. from the nose of the driving cab to the rear vestibule plate.

This glimpse of Pullman luxury was used by the Southern Railway to publicise the provision of cars on Ocean Liner Expresses to Southampton from 1st January, 1931.

Real Photographs

Seating Capacity

Pullman cars provided less seating capacity than normal carriages; in terms of tare weight, around 1¼ tons per passenger. The supplement went to Pullman so did not compensate the railway for carrying this deadweight; however, it must be remembered that the seat occupancy of Pullmans was higher than in normal carriages; on some services up to 100 per cent day after day. In the early cars the seats were distributed sparsely to give an impression of a lounge; thus the parlour car *Princess* had 27 seats, the buffet car *Prince* 26, but the smoking car *Albert Victor*, which was not lounge-like, took 40 persons. The highest numbers were in some of the 3rd class conversions which seated 52 rather austerely, though this was exceeded in the 1932 electric thirds. Buffet and kitchen cars of course seated fewer passengers than parlour cars. There were minor variations from car to car, but seating of some 'standard' cars can be quoted:

    1908:   Brakes 30, parlours 33, buffet 25.
    1910-2:   Buffets 19, parlours 24.
    1921:   12-wheel: parlours 36, kitchens 27.
    1932:   Electric: 1st kitchens 20, 3rd parlours 56, motor 3rds 48, compos 12 1st, 16 3rd.
    1951:   1st parlours 26, 2nd parlours 42, 1st kitchen 22, 2nd brake 36.
    1966:   Parlour 36, kitchen 18, brake 30.

The main change in styling over the years was in the windows. The first (1870s) Pullman design had seven sets of a narrow tall window with smaller ones each side, and two extra end windows. A little later, cars had 17 small windows, and after that four square windows with smaller ones each side and two extra at ends. When cars began to be built in the UK, there were six large windows in the eight-wheelers and seven in the twelve-wheelers, though later the eight-wheelers also had seven windows. There were some exceptions to the above, specially in kitchen cars: some of the latter had one oval lavatory window between the main saloon windows and the kitchen portion, instead of at the ends. The acquired former South Eastern Railway 'American Cars', and cars rebuilt from 1917 ambulance trains (*see later*) differed from the above styles.

The interior of the cars was quite unlike any ordinary carriages in terms of décor and use of materials. It would be tedious to go into the various styles; suffice it to say that the Victorian cars contained much sumptuous but stuffy furnishing, as one would have found in a wealthy drawing room; later a more Edwardian opulence was observable, and towards the end a perhaps healthy trend to simplicity. When new sets of cars were introduced the Press covered the décor rather more fully than the engineering. Much of the terminology is now obscure; for instance in the 1908 'Southern Belle' cars, four were recorded as being in 'Adam' style, two in 'Pergolese' and two in 'French Renaissance' style. Descriptions were full of phrases like 'damask silk' and 'fine mohair velvet', and there is no doubt that such furnishings today would be out of the question.

Naming and Liveries

First class cars were always named and these were used for identification in working timetables. At first royal personages were used, followed by girls' names, precious stones and some romantic places. Some 'courtesy' naming took place: Lord Bessborough, Chairman of the LBSCR, Cosmo Bonsor, General Manager of the SECR, and Lady Dalziel, wife of the Chairman of the 1908 Pullman Company, all had cars named after them.

When third-class cars came in 1915, they were not named, but had 'Car No. X Third Class' on the sides. These 'third class' numbers were not the same as the 'schedule' numbers of the cars, which applied to cars of all classes existing in 1915 or later. In some cases, mostly late conversions or buildings, 'third class' and 'schedule' numbers were the same. From about 1948 the order of words was reversed; that is 'Car No. 15 Third Class' became 'Third Class Car No. 15'; however, from the end of 1949 cars as repainted were lettered only 'Car No. X'. From 1967 all cars only carried their schedule number; some had done so earlier for special reasons. For the boat trains on the SR and LNER some cars were rated 'second class' but it seems that they were not painted 'second class'; full details of second class usage are lacking. By the time third class became second class on BR, on 3rd June, 1956, it is doubtful whether any Pullmans still carried the old class on their sides. Naming made a brief return in 1983.

The original livery was described as brown or mahogany. The word 'Pullman' or 'Pullman Restaurant (or other word) Car' appeared above the windows, with the name of the car in an oval cartouche below the windows. However, the London & South Western Railway (LSWR) cars had 'Pullman Drawing Room Car' on their lower sides. From 1906 livery was entirely different: umber below window level, cream above. 'Pullman' was in elongated gold lettering above the windows, and the name of the car in an ornamented frame of lining; there were coats of arms at each end of the sides. This new livery really only affected the LBSC: there is no photograph known to the author of an LSWR car in the new livery, and the SECR, when they began using Pullmans, had them painted in their own livery of dark lake and gold lining. On the Eastern Section of the SR cars in lake livery were still around as late as 1930. There was a slight change to the standard livery about 1930, the new umber being lighter and the cream darker, with the panels above the windows now umber and not cream.

From 1964 the official livery was changed to light grey with blue stripe along windows; no names were carried. However, few cars appeared in this livery; most were painted in BR colours, blue lower and grey upper, with the name of the train where the car's name had been, and the schedule number on the lower ends.

As detailed later, some cars were painted all-over green or umber for special reasons, and during the last War, while in store, in grey or red lead preservative paint.

Research into Pullman cars can sometimes be confused by the fact that certain names were used more than once; mostly this was a matter of late Eastern Region cars taking names of early SR cars; however, where there may be confusion the names are marked (I) or (II). Another possible cause of difficulty arose from the fact that in 1924/5 eleven cars were built in the UK and shipped to Italy for the use of the Compagnie Internationale des Wagon-Lits (CIWL); they were named *Cynthia, Adrian, Ibis, Hermione, Lydia, Rainbow, Leona, Minerva, Niobe, Octavia, Plato.* All these, except *Hermione,* were returned to the UK in 1928, but only *Adrian, Ibis* and *Lydia* kept their names, the other names having been already re-allotted to other new cars.

As mentioned above, most cars not named after famous people carried names of girls or jewels; a few were named after places far away, such as Leghorn (Livorno); when a car was named *The Arundel* it was found that some passengers thought the car went there and the name was changed.

It can be a fascinating exercise taking any one Pullman car and pondering over its life experience; however, such a survey in print would take up too much space. One thing does seem to appear: that some cars saw a lot more excitement than others. Take the car *Lydia;* she was one of those built in 1925 and immediately shipped to Italy for the CIWL. Of the cars returned in 1928, she was one of the few to keep her name. She then spent some time on the LNER, but was on the 'Bournemouth Belle' after the War; seen on the Special for President Tubman which did a noteworthy Southampton-Harwich run, also on Winston Churchill's funeral train; finally *Lydia* went to the USA in 1968 with the 'Flying Scotsman' tour, and after travelling thousands of miles, remained there for preservation. She probably did a lot of other things too - reports of trains seldom gave the names of the Pullman; certainly there must be other cars which could show equally eventful lives.

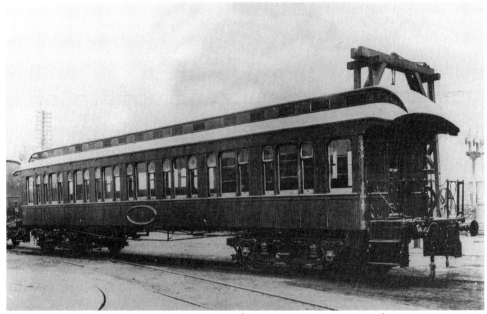

Former American parlour car *Eclipse*, sold to the Midland Railway in 1883, here seen lettered 'Midland Drawing Room Car' and numbered 13.   *H.C. Casserley Collection*

One of the Derby-assembled American Pullman sleeping cars operated by the Midland Railway from 1874, seen here at St Pancras about 1887.   *H.C. Casserley Collection*

Chapter Two

The Derby-Built Cars

Midland Railway

As stated in the last chapter, the early cars were assembled at Derby, and while a few went to other railways, most were for the use of the Midland Railway. The following were the names of the cars, with (in brackets) the number allotted by the MR when it purchased them later:

1874: sleepers, *Midland* (20), *Excelsior* (21), *Enterprise* [note 1];
parlour cars, *Victoria* [note 2], *Britannia* (15, *Windsor* from 1882), *Leo* (14, *Delmonico* from 1882)
1875: sleepers, *St George* (22), *Transit* (24), *Saxon* (25);
parlours, *Ohio* [note 3], *Saturn* (1), *Ocean*
1876: sleepers, *Germania* [note 6], *Australia* [note 7], *Castalia* [note 9], *Scotia* (26), *Italia* (4), *Norman* (27), *India* [note 8], *Minerva* (6)
parlours, *Planet* (7), *Albion* (8), *Comet* (9), *Apollo* (10), *Ariel* [note 4], *Adonis* [note 5].
1877: parlours, *Aurora* (11), *Eclipse* (12), *Alexandra* (13), *Globe* and *Ceres* [note 5]
1882: sleepers, *St Andrew* (28), *St Mungo* (29), *St Louis* (30), St Denis (31)
1883: sleepers, *Missouri* (32), *Michigan* (33)

Notes: 1. Burnt out in Leeds smash, 1882. 2. Passed to LSWR 1880. 3. Later *Prince of Wales*, used on GNR from 1st January, 1879. 4. To LBSCR as *Louise* 1881. 5. *Globe*, to LBSCR as *Beatrice*, *Ceres* as *Maud*, *Adonis* as *Victoria*, all 1881. 6. To Italy after use on MR and GNR. 7. To Wagon-Lits 1883. 8. To GNR 1878. 9. To Italy 1883.

In 1901 the Pullman Co. built four 12-wheeled sleeping cars for the MR (Nos. 34-7), but these were always railway property.

After a trial run with a parlour car in March 1874, from 1st June a regular train was run from St Pancras to Bradford which was at first all-Pullman, but later comprised a third brake at each end, with a 1st/2nd compo in between with a Pullman sleeping car and parlour car. This returned as a day train. On 1st April, 1875 Pullman sleepers were put on the night London-Liverpool train. These cars, sometimes described as drawing-room sleeping cars, had fixed seats like small sofas at the windows, with a removable table in between. The seats drew out to meet each other to provide a lower bunk, and an upper bunk was pulled out from the ceiling, supported on chains. Curtains hanging from the clerestory could be pulled across to shut off the bunks. Passengers did complain of the difficulty in undressing, but on the whole they were popular.

From 1st May, 1876 when the Settle-Carlisle route was open, Pullmans were put on the Scotch expresses. At the same time sleepers were put on the Leeds night run. Day cars, even at this early time included some third class passengers, according to the Revd Clement Brewin of Kettering. By 1881 the Glasgow & South Western Railway, which provided the Scottish end of the Midland, was advertising day and night Pullmans between London and Glasgow.

13

A Pullman sleeper heads a down Midland express near Mill Hill about 1899.

As stated above, the cars were sold to the railway company, but remained labelled Pullmans until 1911, when in view of the fact that they were being used on football excursions, due to their age, this was changed to 'Midland Car'.

These cars were clearly solidly built and lasted well; one was used as a push-pull train on the Wirksworth branch in 1906. Many bodies were grounded as staff huts and had a long life, one being lifted in 1974 from Skipton to Derby for preservation; three were placed at the Midland Railway Trust, Butterley. Another was reframed and ran on a Private railway between Bo'ness and Kinneil.

On 2nd June, 1882 the British Pullman Palace Car Co. was registered as a subsidiary of the American company.

Great Northern Railway

Although the GNR was in the forefront with long distance rail comfort in Victorian days, its involvement with Pullman was brief. The 1875 sleepers *Ohio* and *Ocean* are said to have worked on the GNR from 1875, but the latter was moved to Derby, and it was not until 1879 that a contract was signed to use the former, rebuilt as a day car and renamed *Prince of Wales*, on the Kings Cross to Leeds service. A further sleeper, *India*, had been moved from the MR in 1878; this was destined to be destroyed in the Thirsk collision of 2nd January, 1892.

Two more Derby sleepers, *Columba* and *Iona*, came in 1880; the latter was paired with *Prince of Wales* in a dining car role on the 10 am from Leeds and 5.30 pm from Kings Cross. The *Prince of Wales* still had open balconies, though the other car had closed vestibules; it seems that some sort of wooden footbridge was supplied to bridge the gap between cars.

In 1882 four short sleepers were assembled at Derby; of these *St Denis* and *St Louis* went to the MR and were converted in 1885 from six-wheelers to bogie cars. The other two, *Balmoral* and *Culross*, worked on the GNR from 1883 to 1885, when they were transferred to the Highland Railway (*see below*).

The North Eastern Railway never ran Pullmans as such, but in 1900 one of the Derby Pullman sleepers was rebuilt at York as a day car and run between Leeds and Scarborough, as a tea car for first class, or others by supplement. It carried 'North Eastern Railway Restaurant Car' below the roof, but retained open platforms and the Pullman lozenge in the centre panel. This was presumably a car sold to the GNR and used for a time as East Coast Joint Stock.

Highland Railway

The two six-wheeled sleepers mentioned above were very different from other cars, being only 36 ft 3 in. in length, with centre entrance and four 62 ft compartments with double bunks, a 42 ft vestibule and two lavatories. Some writers have claimed that they could not have been six-wheeled, as Pullmans at that time had no frame to support a centre axle. However it is almost certain that they used the Cleminson system, popular at the time, which comprised

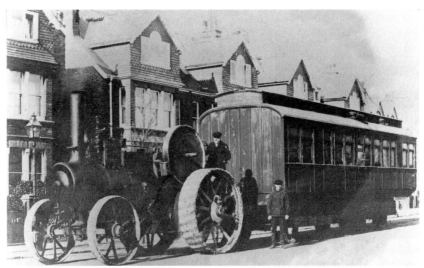

The body of one of the two short Highland Railway sleeper Pullmans, arriving at Seaford in 1918, shortly to become part of a bungalow.   *R.C. Riley*

three inter-acting sub-frames. There could be no other reason for being built so short. They were rebuilt as bogie cars at some time and withdrawn in 1907; they were sent south to the Pullman depot at Brighton, and remained there until 1918, when Mr F. Marks, son of the Pullman General Manager, purchased their bodies and had them built into a bungalow at Seaford. They were forgotten until some detective work by the late Hamilton Ellis found them in the mid-1950s. Recently they were rescued and are to be rebuilt as one car, to be named *Balmoral*. *Culross* had been renamed *Dunrobin* when it moved to the Highland Railway (HR). These cars did not carry the name Pullman, only 'Sleeping Car', but as they were allotted 'schedule numbers' 3 and 4 when these were introduced, it does appear that they were Pullman property.

The cars were worked between Perth and Inverness. In 1907 the HR, irked that the 5s. fee per berth went to the Pullman Co., built new cars comprising first class sleeping quarters and third class seats in bogie carriages 46 ft long. The Pullmans were used in some way on secondary services briefly, before being sent south.

LCDR and LBSCR

The car *Jupiter* is said to have worked on the London Chatham & Dover Railway from 1882-4, but no further Pullman use on that line is recorded, although it did run a Wagons-Lits train for a time. The activities of Derby-built cars on the LBSCR are detailed in Chapter Three.

Chapter Three

South and South-East

Pullmans on the LBSCR

It was on 1st November, 1875 that the first Pullman ran from London (Victoria) to Brighton. This car, named *Mars*, had been obtained from the Midland Railway. The speed of the train was not impressive, the journey taking 70 minutes, with six ordinary carriages attached. This car seems to have stayed on the LBSCR for some time, but was sent to Italy in 1883.

On 5th December, 1881 a complete train of Pullmans was put on, called the 'Pullman Limited Express'. Again the cars were ones assembled at Derby, a few years old: *Victoria* (ex-MR *Adonis*), *Maud* (ex-MR *Ceres*), *Beatrice* (ex-MR *Globe*), and *Louise* (ex-MR *Ariel*); *Maud* was a smoking/luggage car. The train ran every day, but was not popular on Sundays and became weekdays-only for a time. When reinstated on Sundays it was called the 'Pullman Drawing Room Train'. A feature of this stock was that it was electrically lit from batteries charged by a steam engine at Victoria. The cars were finished in mahogany, with the name of the car in a cartouche on the side, and 'Pullman Smoking Car' on the brake car above the windows. One account states that the other cars were lettered 'Drawing Room', 'Parlour' and 'Buffet', but photos suggest they were all lettered 'Restaurant Car'. Two further cars assembled at Derby in 1877 are believed to have been on the line at this time, *Alexandra* and *Albert Edward*, though it is possible they did not arrive until the Midland Railway gave up Pullmans in 1888. *Jupiter*, which had been running on the London Chatham & Dover Railway from 1882, probably came to the LBSC in 1884.

On 11th December, 1888 a new three-car Pullman train began running to Brighton, comprising *Prince* (buffet), *Princess* (ladies) and *Albert Victor* (smoking). This set had side buffers at the outer ends only, the other couplings being of the type later known as 'buck-eye'. Lighting was supplied from a dynamo housed in a six-wheeled LBSC van, painted in Pullman livery (No. 80). Another similar van was built in 1895 (No. 29); these became known as 'Pullman Pups'. Also in 1895 three new cars were supplied: *Her Majesty* (parlour), *Duchess of York* (buffet), *Princess of Wales* (smoking). From 1891 Pullmans were included in the Newhaven boat trains.

The livery at this time was described as 'bronze, gold lines, roof rose, bogies dark brown picked out in yellow'. Photos suggest that not all cars carried their names on the sides.

Ordinary carriages were attached to the Pullmans, though some trains were first-class only. There was to be no all-Pullman train until 1898, when a 'Sunday Pullman Limited Express' was put on. The previous Sunday Pullman had run only in winter, as no path was available for it in the busy summer season, a problem which was to some extent solved by the opening in 1900 of the Redhill avoiding (or Quarry) line. The 'Limited' made the journey in 60 minutes; however, most trains took 75 minutes or more, due to the practice of stopping

L. B. & S. C. Rly. The "Brighton Ltd."

The 'Brighton Pullman Limited' comprising six Derby-built cars with a 'pup' van at each end, No. 29 leading.   *Knight Series 1611*

A Derby-built car of the LBSCR at Newhaven on a boat train about 1905.   *Lens of Sutton*

One of the last of the American cars, *Princess Patricia* (1906) is shown here in the Crumbles siding at Eastbourne. The figure in the centre is Davison Dalziel, who took over the British Pullman Co. in 1907.

Duchess of Norfolk was another of the last USA 12-wheeled cars, and ran as a buffet car. It is seen here on a West Worthing train.   *Lens of Sutton*

"PRINCE OF WALES" L.B.& S.C.R. 3.50 P.M. DOWN PULLMAN L.B. TO BRIGHTON PASSING TOOTING

Only one Pullman set with pup van is on this mixed stock Brighton train near Tooting box about 1902; the cars are still in brown livery, hauled by 'B4' 4-4-0 *Prince of Wales.*

F. Moore

for ticket collection at Preston Park (down) and Grosvenor Bridge (up); also most trains stopped at either East Croydon or Clapham Junction. The famous 5.00 pm from London Bridge (usually called the 'City Limited') took 65 minutes, without ticket stop. The various Pullman trains available included the 9.25 am 'Pullman Drawing Room Car Train' from Brighton, and 'Pullman Limited' trains from Brighton at 1.20 pm and 5.45 pm. Timings and names varied from year to year. By 1898 there were 28 trains on the Brighton line including Pullman cars, the best taking just the hour.

Further Pullmans arrived from America: *The Queen* in 1890, *Pavilion*, *Princess May*, *Duchess of Connaught* and *Prince Regent* in 1893, *Duchess of York* and *Her Majesty* in 1895. In 1899 there was a change to six-wheeled bogies and longer bodies, with *The Arundel* (later *Majestic*), *The Chichester* (later *Waldemar*) followed in 1900 by *Devonshire,* and in 1906 by the last of the American-built cars, *Duchess of Norfolk*, *Princess Ena* and *Princess Patricia.* Meanwhile in 1899 the first Pullman write-off had occurred; *Maud* was virtually destroyed in an accident at Wivelsfield.

Pullmans were now running to Eastbourne, singly or in pairs; however, on Sundays there was a 'Sunday Pullman', although ordinary carriages were also attached. From the summer of 1907 a new 'City Limited' train was running, including three luxurious LBSC saloons vestibuled to a Pullman; one of the saloons had a brake portion housing a dynamo which supplied the whole four-car set; the rest of the train was of normal stock.

The presence of Pullmans in so many trains must have represented an extra burden on the locomotive power. For example, the 5 pm to London from Brighton had two portions, one for Victoria and one for London Bridge, and also took on some through carriages from Worthing. A typical formation noted for this train was: 5 bogies-Pullman-3 bogies-bogie van (for Victoria), van-bogie-Pullman-2 bogies (for London Bridge). It is not mentioned whether it was double-headed. In 1901 the London Bridge portion of this train was still being worked forward from East Croydon by a 'Terrier' 0-6-0T; strange to think of a Pullman behind one of these tiny engines.

Speed as well as comfort was important on the Brighton run. On 26th July, 1903 a 5-car Pullman special behind the 4-4-0 *Holyrood* ran from Victoria to Brighton in 48¾ minutes, said to be the fastest-ever steam run. This compares with an officially-recorded 47 minutes in 1933 with two 6-PUL sets, and an unofficial 43 minutes on another run. It was no doubt with speed in mind that in 1907 Mr Marsh built his special 'I3' class 4-4-2T No. 21, with 6 ft 9 in. driving wheels; however, its performance does not seem to have been anything special, and no more 'big-wheel' 'I3s' were built. Although tender engines were available, the LBSC always seemed to want the Brighton run to be regarded as a tank-engine job. The publicity for the new 1908 'Southern Belle' train showed the stock with an 'I2' class 4-4-2T at its head, though it seems doubtful whether this class could have kept time with a 280-ton load. The later 'J' 4-6-2T and 'L' 4-6-4T classes were tailored for this service and the latter class was still working when electrification came, though as loads grew ever heavier in SR days an infusion of 'King Arthur' 4-6-0s was also necessary.

The year 1907 is a good one to leave the LBSC story for the moment: the 1908 'Belle' was the start of a new era, with the Pullman company under new management. Progress so far had not been impressive for Pullman; there were 27 cars running on the LBSC, but the Midland, Great Northern and Highland had given them up, the LSWR was phasing their few out, and the SECR was running its 'American Cars' independent of Pullman at that time. Perhaps it was only a matter of time. Victorian England was very suspicious of foreign new-fangled ideas, and particularly the notion of sharing a carriage with a lot of other people, even though they be rich and well-behaved, did not appeal. It is interesting that in his book *The Railways of England* published in 1889, W.M. Acworth gives Pullman credit for introducing dining cars and bogie stock, but adds that he personally 'would rather be boxed up in a Midland third class than have the privilege of enjoying the conversation of the public in the most luxurious car Pullman ever fashioned'. The British loved their cramped compartment carriages; the openness of a Pullman took time to get used to.

South Eastern Response

The services to the short-crossing Channel ports must have seemed a natural opportunity for luxury travel ideas, and in 1874 the London Chatham & Dover Railway tried out two 6-wheeled sleeping cars of the Mann Patent Palace Car Co., a fore-runner of the Wagons-Lits company, but they were not a success. The next attempt was with a borrowed Pullman, *Jupiter*, which ran on the LCDR in a 'Dover Pullman Car Boat Train' from 1st July, 1882 to 31st July, 1884, before being returned to the LBSCR. However, when the important Paris Exposition of 1889 came into view it was the Wagons-Lits company who jumped in, arranging with the LCDR for a luxury 'Club Train' to run to Dover in connection with a new 'Calais-Douvres' boat and new terminal at Calais. The train comprised three Belgian day-cars and a fourgon (a baggage/smoking/kitchen car), all painted green. Since the South Eastern Railway was required to pool its Continental receipts with the LCDR, it had to have a similar train; this consisted of two day-cars, a fourgon, and a six-wheeled SER brake-van painted green. From the French end, this seemed to be one train, leaving Paris at 3.30 pm and arriving at Victoria, Charing Cross and Holborn Viaduct at 11.15 pm. From the inclusion of the last-named, it seems that the LCDR train must have stopped at Herne Hill to shed one saloon. Neither company was happy with the financial results, and the trains were taken off on 1st October, 1893. The cars went back to Belgium, though the SER ones were noted as still in Rotherhithe Road sidings in 1895.

Although a semi-official history of the Pullman Company published many years ago refers to a contract having been signed with the LCDR in 1891, there is no record of any further cars on this line until after the LCD/SER fusion. The South Eastern Railway, however, seems to have felt there was a future for luxury trains; but there was to be a difference - the railway would own the cars. In 1891 they ordered from an American builder six cars of Pullman type: four 'drawing room cars' (Nos. 32-5), one buffet car (No. 36)

CHARING CROSS STATION. FOLKESTONE EXPRESS.

This Tuck's postcard shows the South Eastern & Chatham Railway 'Folkestone Car Train' at Charing Cross about 1904; all cars were later taken over by the Pullman company, who rebuilt the brake cars in 1919 as parlour cars *Thistle* and *Albatross* with full length clerestories.

and a luggage car (No. 47), soon converted into another saloon. A special train of these cars was run for the press on 2nd March, 1892 from Charing Cross to Hastings. They had open platforms, but passengers could pass between them over footplates. They were now split up and run singly on various coast trains as first class saloons, no supplement being charged. In 1896 the cars were rebuilt with closed ends; Nos. 32-4 were converted to third class, and No. 36 was second class with an all-class buffet; they were formed into a train, with six-wheeled vans Nos. 283/5, one at each end, all resplendent in red lake gold-lined, and run as 'The Hastings Car Train' from 1st December, 1896. This remained in service for many years; about 1905 the vans were replaced by 3-compartment bogie brakes, at least one of which (No. 2304) was second class.

In 1897 a further eight cars were purchased, from a British builder; first class Nos. 201/2, second class No. 203, third class Nos. 204-6, third brakes Nos. 207/8. One car (No. 171) was also obtained from America. The eight cars formed 'The Folkestone Car Train' which began running in 1897. No. 171 was apparently used for a time on a 'Tunbridge Wells Car Train', and later with two of the other cars, a 'Bexhill Car Train'. The new stock differed from the earlier batch in having brake cars at each end with the clerestory roof over the saloon portion only, and a 'birdcage' end look-out. In 1914 all 15 cars were withdrawn and stored at Blackheath and other places, finally being sold to the Pullman Company in 1919; they returned with little alteration except to the brake coaches, as 'Pullmans' with names as follows:

BOURNEMOUTH EXPRESS, L.&S.W.RY

Pullmans did not last long on the LSWR, and were only used singly on Bournemouth trains; this Pouteau postcard shows a down train headed by two 'T9' 4-4-0s about 1904.

SER No.	Built	Type	Name	SER No.	Built	Type	Name
32	1891	B	Carmen	201	1897	B	Hilda
33	1891	B	Constance	202	1897	P	Dora
34	1891	B	Diana	203	1897	P	Mabel
35	1891	P	Dolphin	204	1897	P	Stella
36	1891	P	Falcon	205	1897	P	Dorothy
47	1891	B	Figaro	206	1897	P	Venus
171	1897	P	Tulip	207	1897	B	Thistle
				208	1897	B	Albatross

B - buffet;   P - parlour

Pullmans on the LSWR

In 1880 the London & South Western Railway borrowed from the LBSC the Pullman car *Alexandra*, and worked it on the Exeter trains, but without much success. However, in 1888 the LSW was seeking ways to popularise the resort of Bournemouth, following the completion of its direct route via Sway, and after various improvements to the service, from 21st April, 1890 a Pullman was added to the 12.30 pm down and corresponding train up. Two cars were obtained, *Duchess of Albany* and *Duchess of Fife*, later joined (1893) by *Princess Margaret* and *Duchess of Connaught*. They were employed singly, and the other stock was not vestibuled in the early years.

In 1906 the LSWR decided upon a policy of using vestibuled trains with dining cars on its best trains; the diners were, however, to be built and owned by themselves, and the Pullmans were progressively set aside from that time. There is some doubt about when the last one ran; some sources place it as late as 1912. However, all did in fact pass to LBSCR service and at least one was there by 1907. *Princess Margaret* was rejected in 1912 as unsuitable and after resting for some time in a siding at Havant, was sent to Longhedge and then back to the LBSC.

No Pullmans ran again on LSWR lines, apart from occasional specials, until 1931.

Progress on the LBSCR and SECR

A new all-Pullman train entitled the 'Southern Belle', which began running on 1st November, 1908 between Victoria and Brighton, broke new ground in many ways. It was the first train, except an earlier Sundays-only one, to make the journey regularly in 60 minutes. The seven cars were all 12-wheelers, British-built, and the first not to have clerestory roofs; being 13 ft 2 in. high, they provided more headroom inside than before or since. Also for the first time food was actually cooked on the train, using a Fletcher-Russell gas cooker (later fitted in most other kitchen cars); up to now, previously-cooked food had merely been kept hot. The train was in the new umber and cream livery, and comprised end-cars *Verona* and *Alberta*, kitchen car *Grosvenor*, and parlour cars

A Pullman special for Brighton 'under the wires' near Balham about 1920. Surprisingly, a nine-car train could be handled by the 1909 'B4' class 4-4-0 No. 54, once named *Princess Royal* and dual-brake fitted.

The Atlantic No. 423 is in LBSC livery, but only the first three cars are from the old twelve-wheeled 'Belle' train the other six being eight-wheelers converted from ambulance cars after the War.

Belgravia, Cleopatra, Bessborough and *Princess Helen*. Each car weighed 40 tons, making a heavy train, but the tare weight per passenger did not work out too badly; the brake cars seated 31, kitchen 25, and parlours 33, total 219. However, an empty run each day was somewhat wasteful; the 5 pm up ran back to Brighton without passengers to form an extra 9 pm up. Also in 1908 an allegedly all-Pullman train to Eastbourne was put on, but it seems at times to have had ordinary carriages attached.

An even greater change was signalled on 12th September, 1915 when the LBSC began including third class Pullmans in two Brighton and one Eastbourne train. The cars were old 'firsts' altered from a lounge-like layout to normal two-by-two seating; the supplement was 9d. The cars carried no name but had 'Car No. X Third Class' on the sides. On 10th September, 1915 the LBSC ran a special train to inaugurate third class Pullmans, calling at Brighton, Worthing and Eastbourne.

The early years of World War I were to some extent 'business as usual' on the railways, but by 1917 it was biting hard, and all Pullmans, apart from three firsts and five thirds on the LBSC, were withdrawn. Some were restored on 1st October, 1919, but the 'Belle' did not return until 1st October, 1921, running twice daily as a two-class train on weekdays, and on Sundays split into a first class and a third class train, both all-Pullman, the latter being referred to as the 'Pullman Limited'.

Meanwhile a contract had been signed with the South Eastern & Chatham management for Pullman cars to supplement their own American cars. Six were supplied, all first class: buffet cars *Corunna, Savona, Sorrento*; parlour cars *Valencia, Florence, Clementina*. They were run in parlour-buffet pairs, though the

A Sunday all-Pullman Brighton train with one of the brake cars rebuilt from an ex-L&Y ambulance car leading; the locomotive is 'I3' class No. 80. *Lens of Sutton*

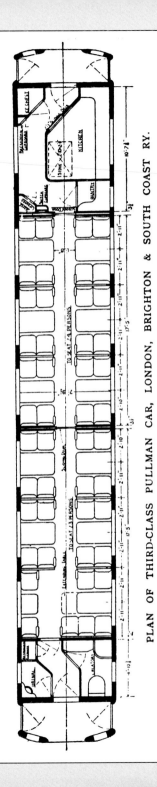

PLAN OF THIRD-CLASS PULLMAN CAR, LONDON, BRIGHTON & SOUTH COAST RY.

The somewhat spartan seating arrangement of one of the new third class cars built in 1921 by Clayton for the Brighton trains; Cars 11-16, all on frames of former LNWR hospital train coaches.

press was first treated to an all-Pullman run in April 1910. They were not finished in normal Pullman livery, but in the standard SECR dark lake with plenty of gold lining. They were eight-wheeled and weighed nine tons less than the LBSC 'Belle' cars, probably just as well in view of the gradients and locomotive power available, *Regina, Sapphire* and *Palermo* came later in 1910. A further car, *Shamrock*, was supplied in 1911 for the Queenborough boat train. In 1912/13 seven more cars came, *Alicante, Cosmo Bonsor, Mimosa, Ruby, Daphne, Topaz* and *Hawthorne*. This enabled Pullmans to be placed on more express trains to the coast, both on the Victoria-Margate-Ramsgate Harbour service, and Charing Cross-Folkestone-Dover-Deal.

The last arrivals before the War were four cars from a batch of 12-wheelers intended for the Caledonian Railway. These Scottish-named cars, *Glencoe, Scotia, Hibernia* and *Orpheus,* are stated to have been placed at the disposal of the War Office for 'top brass' visiting the Front. The first and last were not actually noted on the SR after the War and may have spent a few years elsewhere. Three cars, *Regina, Glencoe,* and *Scotia* formed a Royal train on 31st October, 1919 when the Shah of Persia arrived at Dover.

At the 1920 Pullman Company Annual General Meeting, Sir David Dalziel stated that 'the returns are only limited by the seats available', and 'wider development would only be restricted by the amount of rolling stock they could place at the disposal of the railways'. It was certainly a difficult situation. The company had signed up to provide a number of cars for the Great Eastern Railway (GER), and the engineering industry, being still tooled up mainly for munitions, was not in the best position to build new cars rapidly. Sir David was either lucky or skilful; he was able to take over the 15 'American Cars' of the SECR, which with minimal work were made into Pullmans; he also obtained 22 ambulance carriages from the LNWR, Lancashire & Yorkshire Railway (L&YR) and GWR. All the railways had been asked to make up ambulance trains for moving war wounded to various hospitals, and in most cases the interiors had been so altered that there was no great eagerness to put them back to their original state. It is not certain how much of each vehicle was used, but even if they had to be stripped down to the frames, it was quicker than building completely new cars. In the event, new cars were built for the Great Eastern, the old SER cars were done up a bit for the SECR - though they had less than 10 years' life in them, it was worth while - and the former ambulances, rebuilt during 1921, went out to the LBSCR except for six to the SECR and two to the Caledonian. Of 12 cars from the LNWR, six were rebuilt as first class (*Maid of Kent* (I), *Anaconda, Erminie, Coral, Elmira* and *Formosa*), going to the SECR. All were rebuilt as composites in 1933. The other six became third class Nos. 11- 16 on the LBSC; the L&Y cars (five) became third class Nos. 22-26, and three GWR ones, Nos. 20, 21 and 30, all on the LBSC. Two GWR frames became first class cars on the Caledonian.

There was some attempt to conceal the fact that second-hand vehicles were being used. The description of the ex-LNWR cars in *The Locomotive* in 1921 refers to their being 'built by Clayton'. It says that the use of steel frames (hitherto most cars had been of integral build) was to save weight, and four-wheeled bogies were used for the same reason. It does appear that the bodies were probably all new; however, there was concern over riding qualities; extra

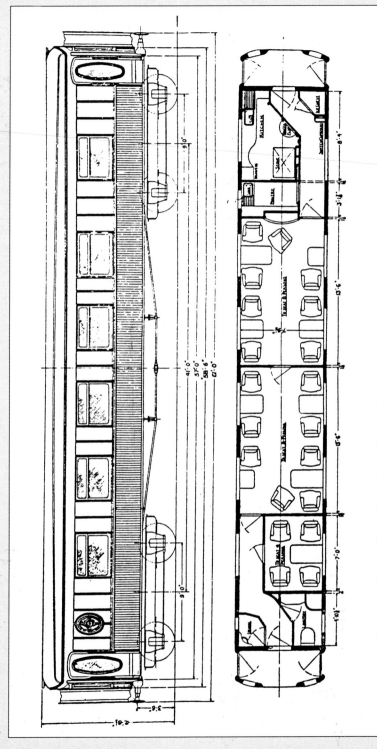

Elevation and plan of *Erminie*, rebuilt by Clayton from an LNWR ambulance car in 1921 and supplied to the SECR.

The SECR's newly-rebuilt 'E1' 4-4-0 No. 163 with a 'special' at Dover Marine about 1920, comprising six of the 1910-1913 eight-wheeled Pullmans.

Lens of Sutton

rubber springs were fitted above the axle-boxes and rubber cushions placed between the frames and the bodies. The cars for the LBSC were finished in normal Pullman livery, but those destined for the SECR were in lake livery.

Some new cars were also being built, 12-wheelers again for the SECR: *Padua* and *Portia* in 1920, *Calais*, *Milan*, *Palmyra* and *Rosalind* in 1921, and *Sylvia*, *Sunbeam*, *Malaga*, *Monaco*, and *Neptune* in 1922. These presented somewhat of a contrast with the converted 'American Cars', some of which were 40 years old, and the weight difference required close attention when making up trains so that permitted tare weight was not exceeded. The old cars soon came off the prestigious Continental runs; one was noted in 1929 still on a main line train, but they were mostly used on specials, the dark lake livery faded to a somewhat curious colour.

The Flushing Boat Train was revived for a short time, until this steamer service was moved to Harwich; it was reported as a short train, three coaches and one Pullman, usually *Regina*. It could be lifted up the steep Folkestone Harbour branch by two 'R' class tank engines, whereas some other trains required five.

The increasing supply of Pullman cars on the SECR enabled them to be put on trains to East Kent; a 'Sunday Thanet Pullman' to Ramsgate began running on 10th July, 1921; this was later a mixed train, which came off finally in 1931. Some of the former SER 'American Cars' were back on the Hastings line by 1922; published figures give the width of both batches of cars as 8 ft 4 in., but this may be an error in respect of the Hastings Car Train, as the Pullmans later built for this service were restricted to 8 ft 1 in., owing to a tight curving tunnel which put this line beyond Tunbridge Wells out of bound for most Pullmans.

From 1921 all services to the Continent except the Flushing service were switched from Charing Cross to Victoria; the area shared by Platforms 1 and 2, on the extreme east side of the station (where in fact the Pullman offices were), became noteworthy for the colourful departure scenes as Pullmans were boarded by top society; it was also later to be the short walk for royalties and notables of all countries between their Pullman Special and the Buckingham Palace landaus waiting in the yard. In 1922 a Pullman was put on the 8.05 am from Margate to Cannon Street and returned on the 5.10 pm from Holburn Viaduct.

It would appear from researches by Mr David Gould that in the early 1920s the SECR had eight trains available for boat train duties. This railway had adopted a policy of having more or less permanently fixed trains; these were given as (for boat trains): Train No. 1, five 12-wheeled Pullmans with first/second brake at each end; No. 2, six coaches, two Pullmans; No. 3, four coaches, three Pullmans; No. 4, four coaches, two 12-wheeled Pullmans; No. 5, five coaches, two Pullmans; No. 6, four coaches, two Pullmans; No. 7, three coaches, two Pullmans; No. 8, two coaches, one Pullman. Trains Nos. 1 and 2 were all-gangwayed, others had some gangwayed carriages. However, the exigencies of service caused much second-rate stock to appear on boat trains, even after the construction of new stock set in hand by the SECR had been completed in 1924. It may seem remarkable that the SECR could allot 19 Pullmans to the boat trains, find 16 for Epsom Races, and still cover all other commitments.

Chapter Four

The Great Eastern and LNER (GE Section)

The Great Eastern Railway (GER) decided to run Pullmans after World War I, perhaps because some of its East Coast resorts shared the same kind of residents and visitors as Eastbourne and Brighton. Six cars were built for them by Clayton in 1920, third class cars 45 and 47, second class 56/7, and first class *Ansonia* and *Arcadia*. The schedule numbers were 106-9, but for some reason Car 45 was 17 and Car 56 was 173. The contract was for 10 cars, and later the same year first class cars *Cambria* (119), *Catania* (120) and *Corsair* (126) were supplied; also third class car 46 (110), added.

The cars were 63 ft 10 in. over vestibules (66 ft 11½ in. over buffers); the width was 8 ft 10 in. and the 12 ft wheelbase bogies were at 41 ft centres. The first class cars seated 21, and included a pantry; each was finished in a different interior style. Cooking was by gas, and Stone's lighting was employed, also Laycock heating. The second and third class cars seated 47. There was a need for second class cars, because the Pullmans were to be used on the 'Hook Continental' trains, and the GER suffered with the SECR from a proportion of through passengers from the Continent with second class tickets. It is not certain that 'Second Class' appeared on the cars, though the third class ones were clearly lettered 'Third Class Car No. _'.

By 1922 the Great Eastern had managed to get either restaurant cars or Pullmans back on to all their good trains. One train had both, the 8.15 am from Liverpool St, with a Pullman for Cromer and a restaurant car for Yarmouth. Other Pullman workings were two third class cars to Cromer, one each first and third to Cambridge and to Norwich via Cambridge; also one to Bury St Edmunds and two to Hunstanton. There were also the boat trains; the Pullmans were first class to Parkeston Quay but first and second to Harwich Town for the Hook of Holland. Cars 56/7 were second class, but were converted to third in 1923.

On 16th July, 1922 the Great Eastern began running the 'Clacton Belle', leaving Liverpool St at 10 am and running non-stop to Clacton, arriving at 11.37. This was a light train, two first class and four third class cars, easily handled by a 'Claud Hamilton' 4-4-0. At Grouping the Great Eastern had the use of 15 Pullmans.

In 1924 there was a reduction in the number of cars; the LNER had decided to extend the use of all-Pullman trains on the former Great Northern and needed 'end cars'; the LBSC system of running bogie brakes as required on the 'Belle' apparently did not appeal. So two 12-wheeled firsts, *Ansonia* and *Arcadia*, and four thirds, Cars 46, 57, 40 and 41 were sent to Longhedge to be converted to brake cars with large luggage spaces, thereafter being transferred to Kings Cross services.

On 30th March, 1925 a new 'Hook Continental' began running; it comprised a second brake, three seconds, kitchen, restaurant, then three first class cars, a first and a second Pullman, and two vans.

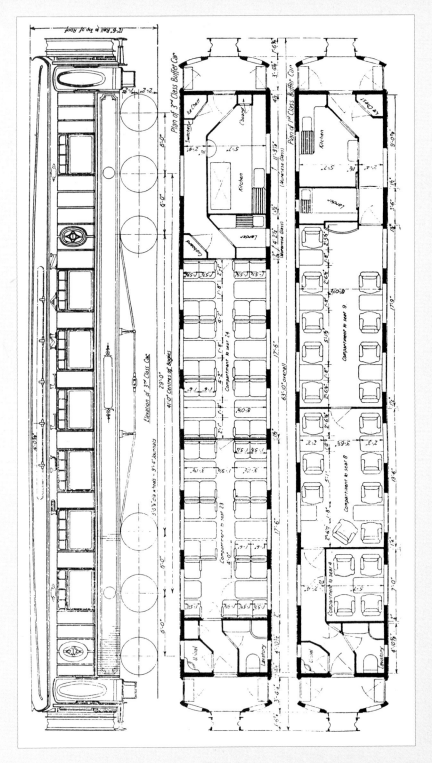

Elevation and plans of first and third class Pullman cars, Great Eastern Railway, 1920.

Twelve-wheelers predominate on this 'Clacton Belle' hauled by 4-4-0 No. 8783.

On 3rd June, 1929 the LNER began running an extension of the 'Belle' trains; the train ran to a different destination each day, often on schedules faster than the normal ones. In 1929 the destinations were Monday, Felixstowe; Tuesday, Clacton; Wednesday, Frinton and Walton; Thursday, Dovercourt and Harwich; Friday, Thorpeness and Aldeburgh. By 1934 destinations were wider: Sunday, Clacton; Monday, Wroxham, North Walsham, Cromer; Tuesday; Thorpeness Halt and Aldeburgh; Wednesday, Clacton again; Thursday, Wroxham, West Runton and Sheringham; Friday, the longest run, Skegness in 3 hrs 25 mins. The make-up varied from six to eight cars, but always included one 'first'. In 1936 5-day Belle 'seasons' were offered, 25s. third class and 37s. 6d. first, the former representing a rate of three miles per penny. By now these trains were usually hauled by the 'Sandringham' class 4-6-0s. Occasional visits were also made to Cambridge, Hunstanton and Lowestoft. From 8th July, 1929 Pullmans replaced the restaurant cars on the Flushing boat trains, though no Pullman supplement was charged.

A new 13-coach train was put on the 'Hook Continental' service from 3rd May, 1936; it was a three-class train, but it seems that the two Pullman cars on it were both first class.

Pullmans continued in use on the Continental trains of the former GER until World War II. Pullman cars returned to the Boat Trains later in the 1970s, but not as real Pullmans; they were described as 'first class opens' and of course ran in BR livery. There were four or five on each train; they were laid aside as new open coaches arrived.

The up 'Clacton Belle' on the Great Eastern section of the LNER, leaving Clacton about 1929 hauled by a 'Super-Claud' 4-4-0.   *H. Gordon Tidey*

Chapter Five

The Caledonian and Some Small Users

Caledonian Railway

This company made ambitious plans for the use of Pullmans in 1914, but because of the outbreak of War they were not fully implemented at that time. Seventeen cars were ordered: four dining cars for three services between Glasgow and Aberdeen, 12 buffet cars for seven trains between Glasgow and Edinburgh, and buffets for what later became the 'Tinto' from Glasgow to Moffat and 'Strathearn' to Crieff, and an observation car.

Three cars, *Flora Macdonald, Fair Maid of Perth*, and *Lass of Gowrie* were in service between Glasgow and Aberdeen in August 1914, also a Pullman observation car, *Maid of Morven*, on the Oban service. This car was only 59 ft 4½ in. overall, compared with the others at 63 ft 10 in., and ran on four-wheeled bogies while they were 12-wheeled. The rear half was glazed, including the rear bulkhead, with rear-facing seats. The other end of the car was of normal design, with a buffet and lavatories.

Three more cars, *Mary Beaton, Mary Hamilton*, and *Annie Laurie*, seem to have gone into service early in the War. As late as 1916 the Caledonian was promoting its Pullmans to Perth and Aberdeen, and four first class buffets (six on Saturdays) between Glasgow and Edinburgh. Passengers from Edinburgh could join the northbound Pullman at Larbert, Stirling or Perth, and those bound for Edinburgh from the North could leave their cars at Perth or Larbert, depending on which train was involved.

Three cars arrived in 1919 which had been built before the War, but probably not delivered: *Mary Seaton, Mary Carmichael* and *Helen McGregor*. By 1922 there were enough cars to run an all-Pullman train for a time between Glasgow and Edinburgh. Most of the buffet cars were two-class, but those on the Edinburgh service remained first class until after Grouping.

From June 1922 a Pullman diner was attached to the 10.10 am from Glasgow to Aviemore on the Highland Railway. Also on 10th July the Great North of Scotland put one on the 8.05 am Aberdeen to Inverness, which ran over the HR between Elgin and Inverness. The Glasgow & South Western Railway (GSWR) also made use of the Pullmans before and after Grouping. These were announced simply as diners, but photographs show Pullmans on the 8.25 am Ayr to Glasgow and 5.10 pm return. These were 'no luggage' trains for commuters.

The Pullmans running on the Caledonian in 1922 included breakfast cars on the part of the journey from Carlisle of the 11.00 pm Euston to Aberdeen and 11.40 pm Euston to Glasgow; also a tea car on the 1.30 pm Glasgow to Aberdeen, and between Symington and Perth off the 10.00 pm Euston to Aberdeen. The Observation Pullman *Maid of Morven* left Glasgow at 10.10 am and returned on the 3.50 pm from Oban. A large proportion of available cars were run between Glasgow and Edinburgh; they were on trains leaving Glasgow at 8.40, 9.50, 11.00 am, and 1.35, 4.00, 5.05 and 6.45 pm. That on the last train remained overnight at Edinburgh and returned on the 6.20 am from

THE CALEDONIAN RAILWAY

PULLMAN CARS.

PULLMAN CARS, the property of the Pullman Car Company, Limited, are run on certain Sections of the Caledonian Railway.

PULLMAN DINING CARS.

Glasgow (Buchanan Street), Perth, and Aberdeen.

These Cars are provided with First and Third Class accommodation, and Passengers travelling by the following Trains will be admitted to the First Class and Third Class section of the Cars (according to the class of Ticket held) for Meals or other refreshments without payment of any supplementary fare:—

TO THE NORTH.

Breakfast Car—7.20 a.m. Express, Glasgow (Buchanan Street) to Perth, Dundee (West), and Aberdeen.

Luncheon Car—10.0 a.m. Express, Glasgow (Buchanan Street) to Perth, Inverness, and Aberdeen.

Tea and Dining Car—5.0 p.m. Express, Glasgow (Buchanan Street) to Perth, Dundee (West), and Aberdeen.

Passengers from Edinburgh (Princes Street) to the North by 7.0 a.m. Train may join the Breakfast Car at Larbert, those by 9.25 a.m. Train may join the Luncheon Car at Perth, and those by 4.25 p.m. Train may join the Tea and Dining Car at Larbert, Stirling, or Perth.

FROM THE NORTH.

Luncheon Car—10.5 a.m. Express from Aberdeen (12.24 p.m. from Perth).

Luncheon and Tea Car—1.10 p.m. Express from Aberdeen (3.52 p.m. from Perth).

Tea and Dining Car—5.30 p.m. Express from Aberdeen (7.43 p.m. from Perth).

Passengers for Edinburgh (Princes Street) by 10.5 a.m. and 5.30 p.m. Trains from Aberdeen may use the Cars from Aberdeen to Perth, and those by 1.10 p.m. Train may use the Car on that Train from Aberdeen to Larbert.

PULLMAN BUFFET CARS.

Glasgow (Central) and Edinburgh (Princes Street).

From GLASGOW (Central).

9.50 and 11.0 a.m., 1.30, 2.20 (Saturdays only), 4.5, and 5.10 p.m. (Saturdays only).

From EDINBURGH (Princes Street).

9.0 a.m., 12.55, 2.20 (Saturdays only), 3.55, 4.55, and 9.50 p.m. (Saturdays only)

The Buffet Cars are available for First Class Passengers only, on payment of a supplementary charge of 1s. for each seat occupied, in addition to the ordinary First Class fare.

The Pullman Car Company provide in their Buffet Cars, for sale to passengers, an extensive variety of food and refreshments, including Wines, Spirits, Liqueurs, and Aerated Waters of the best quality.

Application for reserved seats in the Pullman Buffet Cars should be made to the Station Master at the starting point of the train, and Pullman Car tickets will be issued at the Booking Office at the starting point and at the principal Stations on the journey, and also by the Conductor on each Car.

The number of tickets issued will be strictly limited to the number of seats in the Cars.

The Conductors who travel with these Cars will be authorised to reserve seats for passengers making previous application for them, and passengers travelling by the Cars who have not reserved seats beforehand will not be permitted to occupy seats already secured by other passengers.

Tickets available to travel by the Pullman Cars will be issued subject to these conditions.

The holder of a Pullman Car ticket by accepting it agrees that it is issued subject to the Bye-Laws, Regulations, and Conditions in the Time Tables and Notices of the Caledonian Railway Company and all other Companies or Owners on whose Railways, Coaches, or Vessels the ticket is available, and subject to the further condition that the respective Companies and Owners are not to be liable for any loss, damage, injury, delay, or detention caused or arising off their respective Railways, Coaches, or Vessels, the Contract and liability of each Company or Owner being limited to their own Railways, Coaches, or Vessels.

The Pullman Car Company, Limited, and the Caledonian Railway Company hereby give notice that they decline to accept responsibility for articles of luggage which passengers may take with them into the Pullman Cars. Such articles are only admitted into the Cars for the convenience of passengers, who are expected to exercise the same personal care of them as in an ordinary railway carriage, and the Conductors of the Cars are not permitted to accept any responsibility for their safe custody. DONALD A. MATHESON, General Manager.

FEBRUARY, 1916.

The Caledonian Railway's observation Pullman *Maid of Morven* at Stirling in LMS days at the rear of the afternoon up train from Oban; it will come off at Glasgow, and needed turning at each end of its journey. The date is 31st July, 1936.   *Author*

The ex-LMS Pullman *Queen Margaret* having its kitchen 'gassed up' at The Mound, after working from Inverness in BR days, now Refreshment Car No. 219.

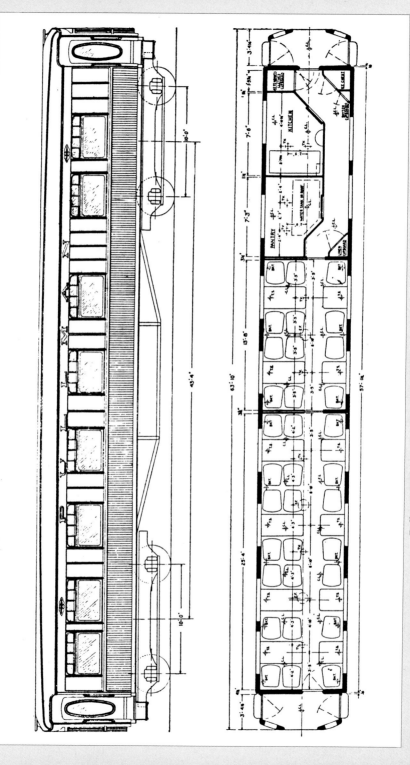

Pullman dining car, *Meg Dods*, LMSR (Caledonian Section), 1923.

there. Similarly the last Pullman to arrive at Glasgow, on the 7.05 pm from Edinburgh, stayed at Glasgow for the 8.40 am next day. Formerly first class only, by 1932 all cars on this route were composites.

The newly formed London, Midland & Scottish Railway (LMS) took over as the pre-War Caledonian programme was being completed. Two 8-wheeled cars using GWR ambulance frames were added in 1922: *Lady Nairn* and *Bonnie Jean*. Four more new cars were ordered for the ex-Caledonian and GSWR services: first class diners *Meg Dods*, *Lass of Ballochmyle* and *Mauchline Belle*; also third class buffet Car No. 80. These Clayton cars were 66 ft over buffers and had 10 ft bogies with Caledonian features.

Some 12-wheeled kitchen cars were rebuilt as dining cars at Longhedge for the LMS in 1927: *Jenny Geddes* (formerly *Nevada*), *Diana Vernon* (former *Atlanta*) and *Jeanie Deans* (former *Columbia*). In the same year Metropolitan delivered three more 12-wheelers: *Queen Margaret*, *Kate Dalrymple* and *Helen of Mar*.

In 1933 all 22 cars working on the LMS in Scotland were sold to the railway, working as before but in LMS livery and without names. There was one exception; the observation car *Maid of Morven* remained in Pullman livery on the Oban service, without the word 'Pullman' but with its number 209 above the name, which was retained. The sale included *Duchess of Gordon*, which had worked on the SECR as *Shamrock*.

Great Western Railway

The GWR was not able to take part in the early enthusiasm for Pullmans as most of its important trains remained broad gauge. Later, in 1921, the Bath Council asked for a Pullman train, but was refused. Nevertheless in 1929 a Pullman train named the 'Torquay Pullman' was put on, serving Paignton also. It first ran on 8th July, using the cars *Eunice*, *Juana*, *Zena* (parlours), *Ione*, *Joan*, *Loraine*, *Evadne* (kitchen cars); they were traditional cars built by Metropolitan Carriage & Wagon. Some had been put into service somewhat earlier, in May 1929, on Plymouth Boat Trains.

The new train departed from Paddington at 11.00 am and reached Paignton at 2.50 pm. The return was ten minutes slower. The GWR management appears to have deliberately sabotaged the service by putting on their own 'Torbay Express' which was faster and of course did not require a supplement to the fare. Not surprisingly, the Pullman was taken off next year, and the cars redirected to the Southern Railway, mainly on Southampton Boat Trains.

In 1955, by which time the persons with a dislike of Pullmans had departed, a new 'South Wales Pullman' was put on, the 9.55 am from Paddington to Swansea calling at Newport, Cardiff, Port Talbot and Neath. The rake used included the 'Daffodil Bar', which was the former 1928 car *Diamond*. From 11th September, 1961 the locomotive-hauled train was replaced by a diesel 'Blue Pullman' set (*see later*) which knocked half-an-hour off the schedule and added a stop at Bridgend. The new train differed from the old one in running up in the morning and back in the afternoon.

An unusual Pullman working on the WR occurred on 17th October, 1965, when a train of seven cars carried travellers joining a cruise ship at Falmouth.

Mayflower was one of two cars built by Birmingham C&W for use by the Metropolitan Railway in 1910, without vestibules, as it was intended to run them singly on business trains between the City termini and Aylesbury. It is seen here in 1936 in the lake livery preferred by Sir Edward Watkin, though they originally ran in standard livery.   *H.C. Casserley*

The Great Southern Railway of Ireland took on four Pullmans in 1926, using them singly as diners on trains from Dublin to Cork, Limerick and Sligo. This photograph was taken about 1929.   *R. Murphy*

The Metropolitan Railway

The Metropolitan Railway was very conscious of its wealthy passengers in Buckinghamshire, and in 1910 decided to improve their travel conditions by ordering from Birmingham Carriage & Wagon two Pullman cars, of the standard design but without vestibules, as it was intended to run them individually. They were named *Galatea* and *Mayflower*, and ran in chocolate and cream livery until the memory of Sir Edwin Watkin caused them to be changed to dark red used by the SE&CR. They were 59 ft 6 in. over the body, and seated 19, in three compartments taking eight, seven and four persons respectively.

The first ran on 1st June, 1910 on a morning train from Aylesbury to Aldgate, non-stop from South Harrow to Baker Street. The Pullman was only available to first class passengers, at an extra fare of 6*d.* from Rickmansworth or 1*s.* from Aylesbury. Breakfast was served on the 8.26 am from Aylesbury, which soon terminated at Liverpool St, and a supper train was put on for theatre-goers leaving Baker Street at 11.35 pm, arriving at Aylesbury at 12.52 am.

Over the years the service changed at times, some trains starting from Chesham or Quainton Road, and some terminating at Baker Street. On Saturdays in 1931 for example the business trains ran at mid-day, 12.58 from Liverpool Street for Aylesbury and 1.34 for Chesham.

In the first few years the Pullman trains were steam-worked as far as Harrow, but from 5th January, 1925 the change to electric haulage was made at Rickmansworth.

The cars were taken off in 1940 and sent to Hampton Court for stabling; it seems that in due course their bodies were used for bungalows.

Great Southern of Ireland

Four cars were provided in 1926 for Irish Pullman Ltd, the bogies for the Irish gauge of 5 ft 6 in. being provided by the LMSR (Northern Counties Committee) (NCC). They were however not run on the NCC, but on the Great Southern Railway (GSR), between Dublin and Cork, Limerick and Sligo. They were 62 ft 4 in. unclassed kitchen cars, numbered 100-3 in the Schedule, weight 39½ tons, seating 46, and with gas cooking.

The cars became GSR property in 1937, but continued running in Pullman livery. By 1938 they were referred to as 'restaurant cars' and ran additionally to Westport and Athlone. They were not used during World War II, and when restored in 1946, ran in green livery. By 1960 only No. 100 was in use, and this later became a service vehicle at Inchicore Works.

Rosemary was one of four eight-wheeled cars built by the Midland RC&W in 1923 for LNER service; however in fact all turned up later on the SR.

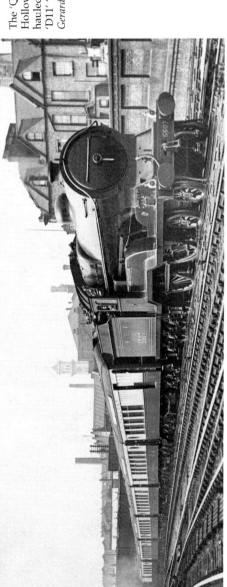

The 'Queen of Scots' on Holloway Bank about 1929, hauled by ex-Great Central 'D11' 'Director' class 4-4-0 *Gerard Powys Dewhurst.*

F.R. Hebron

Chapter Six

Pullman Trains Out of Kings Cross

The newly-created London & North Eastern Railway in 1923 came to an early decision that Pullman cars were not remunerative on the former Great Eastern, apart from the Boat Trains, and transferred most of them to the Great Northern line. As early as 9th July, 1923 the 'Harrogate Pullman', an all-Pullman train, began running from Kings Cross. There was no doubt that the spa town had the right sort of visitors for a luxury train. Curiously, this rake of six cars hauled by an Atlantic type engine was exactly the same in appearance as the long-established and successful 'Southern Belle' between Victoria and Brighton.

The train served Leeds also, and was soon extended to Newcastle. From 21st September, 1925 it was extended further, to Edinburgh, and its route altered to run via Shafteholme Junction and Knottingley (over LMS metals) rather than via Leeds. A separate Pullman train was put on for Leeds and Bradford.

The popularity of the train was partly due to accelerated timings; the 185 mile non-stop run to Leeds was done in 205 minutes; under the new routing the non-stop run was even longer, from Kings Cross to Harrogate. In February 1927 a trial was made on this train of an ex-Great Central 4-4-0 *Marne* to replace the GNR Atlantic, and from now on ex-Great Central 4-4-0 and 4-6-0 engines were seen on many Pullman workings.

The 'Leeds and Bradford Pullman' had its first run on 21st September, 1925, at 11.10 am from Kings Cross; the Edinburgh train left at 11.20. To avoid confusion, from early 1927 the 11.10 was named the 'West Riding Pullman'. After a short period being referred to as the Harrogate & Edinburgh Pullman, the 11.20 was officially named 'Queen of Scots'. The 'West Riding' had been given an extra stop at Wakefield (Westgate) in 1926, where cars for Bradford and Halifax were detached. The timing was now altered, the morning run being in the up direction, leaving Newcastle at 9.15 am and returning from Kings Cross at 4.45 pm; it now called at Darlington, Ripon, Harrogate, Leeds and Wakefield. The up train arrived at Kings Cross at 3.00 pm, giving a lay-over of less than two hours; the Pullman set ran 567½ miles each day, very good utilisation for those times.

The Leeds route was somewhat heavier going than that via Knottingley; there was a half a mile of 1 in 100 out of Leeds to Holbeck, then ⅜ mile at 1 in 50. For down trains there was the long Stoke Bank, 5½ miles at 1 in 200.

Success was not automatic; a 'Sheffield Pullman' had been tried from 2nd July, 1924, running over the former Great Central route to Sheffield (Victoria) via Nottingham. It did not attract traffic and was altered to run via Retford to Manchester instead of Nottingham; but it was discontinued in 1925.

Three kitchen cars built by Metropolitan Carriage & Wagon were added in 1927: *Marcelle, Sybil* and *Kathleen*. Midland C&W supplied third class cars 59-64 (Nos. 62 and 64 were for a time reclassed second for Harwich boat trains).

Ex-GCR 4-6-0 *Earl Haig* heads the 'Harrogate Pullman' near Potters Bar with one of the Birmingham brake Pullmans 40/1 leading.

F.R. Hebron

The down 'Harrogate Sunday Pullman' at Crumple Beck, Harrogate about 1931. The engine is
ex-NER 'D21' class No. 1243. *R.W. Airy*

The up 'Queen of Scots' passes Princes Street Gardens, Edinburgh in August 1932, hauled by
'Director' class 4-4-0 *Edie Ochiltree*. *C.J.L. Romanes*

The up 'West Riding' passing the Stray at Harrogate about 1932, hauled by ex-NER Atlantic No. 710.   *R.W. Airy*

The up 'Queen of Scots' on Lucker troughs in April 1932, hauled by ex-NER Pacific *City of Durham*.   *H.R. Denton*

A rare view of the short-lived 'Sheffield Pullman' near Kirkby, hauled by an ex-GCR four-cylinder 4-6-0 *Earl Beatty*. *F.R. Hebron*

The 'Queen of Scots' near Knebworth on 25th September, 1931; the engine has the unwieldy name of *Gerard Powys Dewhurst*. *R. Brookman*

'A1' Pacific *Dick Turpin* on the down 'Queen of Scots' passing Reston in August 1932.

C.J.L. Romanes

In 1928 two new trains of all-steel stock were built for the 'Queen of Scots' by Metro, made up as follows: brake, 3rd buffet, 1st parlour, 1st buffet, 3rd parlour, 3rd buffet, brake. They were all eight-wheeled cars, 63 ft 10 in. overall, 8 ft 7 in. wide, with 10 ft bogies at 43 ft 4 in. centres. Third class cars were numbered 67-80, or which 77-80 were brakes. The first class cars were named *Nilar, Belinda, Sheila, Thelma, Phyllis, Agatha, Penelope, Ursula, Lucille.*

In 1930 the ending of the 'Torquay Pullman' made some further cars available, though most went onto the Southampton boat trains. Of the third class cars, Nos. 81-4, the last two must have been on the LNER in 1939 as they were leased by the LNER and ran in brown livery as Nos. 483/4.

Many Pullmans had no rest at week-ends, as the 'Sunday Harrogate Pullman' was a popular train, which also served Bradford. It left Kings Cross at 10.30 am and returned there at 7.15 pm.

Not all cars in Scotland worked to London. One ran between Edinburgh (Waverley) and Perth by the LNER route. This left Edinburgh at 7.30 am with the Perth portion of the 'Night Scotsman', returning at 12.25 pm attached to the through coach which would attach to the 2.05 pm Edinburgh to Kings Cross. It went out again at 4.31 pm and was back again from Perth at 8.10 pm on the up 'Highlandman'. Another car did two return workings from Edinburgh to Glasgow, and in summer also worked the 'Lothian Coast Express' between Glasgow and North Berwick.

Now that it was running all-Pullman trains, the LNER was faced with the absence of end-cars to carry luggage. At first vans were run with some trains, but this did spoil the appearance. Therefore some 12-wheeled cars were taken from the ex-GER service and rebuilt with generous luggage space. *Ansonia* and *Arcadia* were given luggage compartments 23 ft 8 in. long for the 'Harrogate Pullman' and 22 ft for the 'Queen of Scots', while third class cars 46, 56 and 57 had even larger space, 33 ft 10 in.; cars 40 and 41 for the 'Sheffield Pullman' had only 22 ft. No vestibule connection was provided at the brake end. In 1934 *Ansonia* and *Arcadia* were demoted from first brake to third brake, numbered 94/5.

In 1935 the LNER devised a new type of prestige train, the 'Silver Jubilee' between London and Newcastle, comprising their own silver-liveried stock. As a result the 'West Riding Limited' no longer served Newcastle, and was renamed the 'Yorkshire Pullman'; the southbound morning working ran via York, which had not had Pullmans before; it now joined cars from Hull at Doncaster. The afternoon return was via Leeds. Engines were now drawn from Doncaster shed, and as the 'Queen of Scots' was worked by Leeds men, the 'Pullman link' at Kings Cross, which had handled the trains from 1923, had no further part. The 'Yorkshire Pullman' was normally nine cars, but sometimes more, and did not always keep time.

In 1937 the 'West Riding Limited' was reborn as a blue streamlined train, similar to the 'Coronation'; a supplement was charged as had been the case with the Pullman trains.

The LNER was not able to restore Pullman trains after the War as rapidly as the SR did; its stock was dispersed and some had been taken into ordinary stock and repainted. However the 'Yorkshire Pullman' got going again from 4th

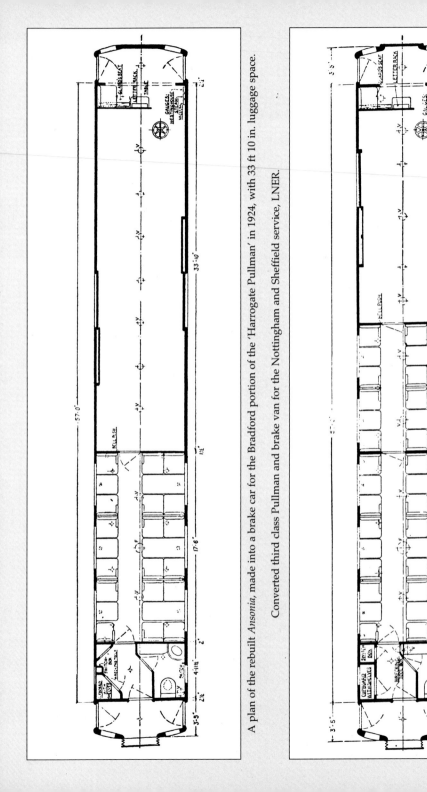

A plan of the rebuilt *Ansonia*, made into a brake car for the Bradford portion of the 'Harrogate Pullman' in 1924, with 33 ft 10 in. luggage space.

Converted third class Pullman and brake van for the Nottingham and Sheffield service, LNER.

The 'Tees-Tyne Pullman' in British Railways days, with 'A4' Pacific *Walter K. Whigham* near Hadley Wood; note the elaborate lining out of the end coach.   *British Railways*

The 'Yorkshire Pullman' at a time when it was made up to ten cars, hauled by 'A2' Pacific *Trimbush*.   *Lens of Sutton*

November, 1946, with class 'A3' Pacifics hauling nine cars, only to be withdrawn for a while the following February owing to the fuel crisis. The Hull portion, normally four cars, was hauled for many years up to 1959 by the rather pretty class 'D49' 4-4-0s, from Doncaster.

The 'Queen of Scots' did not come back until 5th July, 1948, ten cars of which two were detached at Leeds. The 'Tees-Tyne' began again from 27th September, 1948, a day-trip train arriving at Kings Cross a 2.16 pm and leaving at 5.30. Pullman attendants could arrange cars to meet the passengers to make the most use of the three hours available to them.

On 15th September, 1958 an all-Pullman 'Master Cutler' began running from Kings Cross, replacing a train from Marylebone to Sheffield. Eight old cars were used until replaced in 1960; from 1962 Brush diesel locomotives hauled it. From 1965 the train ran to Sheffield Midland rather than Victoria; a stainless steel headboard was presented by the Company of Cutlers. Old-type end-cars topped and tailed the 1960 cars until 15th April, 1966, when the whole train reverted to non-Pullman stock; from 7th October of that year the London terminus became St Pancras (*see Chapter Eight for details*).

The 'Master Cutler' at Werrington Junction in July 1959, the six-car train being easy work for the new type '4' diesel locomotive No. D206.   *D.C. Ovenden*

Chapter Seven

The Southern Railway
and BR (Southern Region)

Although the new Southern Railway followed the LSWR in most things, it did not follow it in turning its back on Pullmans. The use of these cars was extended on the SECR and LBSCR and brought back to the LSWR main line after an absence of 20 years. Somewhat oddly, the livery was not at first standardised, so that some Pullmans remained in lake livery on the Eastern Section until about 1930, and one or two in this livery strayed on to the Central Section. The SR took over the working of a fleet of 110 cars. They were a mixed bunch; most of the ex-LBSC American-built cars were still running, so that clerestory roofs mingled with domed roofs even on the 'Southern Belle'; the refurbished 'American Cars' of the old SER were also running, with their clerestory roofs; there were also old and new 12-wheelers, though no more were built after 1923.

By 1922 rich people were moving about as never before, but the carriage builders had barely recovered from their War work, and there was a big backlog of Pullman cars under construction. The only railway which had anything like enough cars was the LBSC, which was able to provide 12 Pullman trains daily to Brighton alone: two 'Belles', two morning third class, and eight first/third, all from Victoria. In addition, there were two for Portsmouth (one from London Bridge) and a business train terminating at Angmering, whose Pullman came back to London next morning on the 8.17 am from that station; also one to Eastbourne and two Newhaven Boat Trains.

The SECR meanwhile, awaiting new Pullmans and also its own 'American Cars' converted to Pullmans, had to place its cars on the boat trains apart from two daily workings to Deal. Officially the continental trains were the 9.15 am all classes to Dover and the similar 8.00 pm. However, many reliefs had to be run; loadings on these trains were far from predictable, and a passenger wanting a Pullman seat was not going to be satisfied with anything else, unlike the ordinary passenger, who hardly knew a bogie coach from a six-wheeler, and not only did not expect to dine, but had probably decided to do without a lavatory.

Up to now there had been very little movement of cars between railways; the number series for third class LNER cars was started at 40, although the LBSC series ended at 36, and no car numbered over 36 was to stray on to the SR until 1931. With first class cars, there was no apparent demarcation - except that the Caledonian cars had very Scottish names - and no history of Pullmans has made clear in all cases what railway the cars were built for. An official photograph of four cars built in 1923 by Midland Carriage & Wagon has written on the back 'built for the LNER', but two of them (*Iolanthe* and *Rosemary)* were noted on the SR in 1927. It therefore seems worth while to quote the list of Pullmans noted by the author running on the Southern Railway in 1927/8, even though it appears that a few were missed (listed at the end). It is perhaps difficult for readers of today to realise how long the idea of separate railways lasted into the grouping era; an ex-LBSC Pullman on the former SECR would have been a great event (though not very likely, as many were outside the SECR gauge). All the same, there must have

On 1st January, 1925 the SR announced a 'new' 'Southern Belle', and it is seen here on the 5th near Quarry Box; but the stock is in fact old and the use of a bogie brake instead of the former brake/parlour car a retrograde step.

O.J. Morris

This Eastbourne train crossing the River Ouse at Southerham Junction contains the bar-car *Myrtle* and another 1908 car; the date is 17th July, 1934.

O.J. Morris

been some interesting cases, which were not observed by the then small band of railway observers, for three of the massive 'Hook Continental' 12-wheelers of the former GER visited Longhedge Works in 1924 for rebuilding. Did they take the direct route via Shadwell and Peckham Rye, or some other? It is strange that record in the magazines of non-revenue movement of Pullmans is almost non-existent. All the cars in the following table were noted working in trains, and not in sidings or workshops, which explains why they are not quite complete.

Table One - Pullmans noted running on the SR in 1927/8

A: on Eastern Section. B: on Central Section. Bk: with luggage or guard section. K: with Kitchen or Buffet. L: running in red lake livery. P: Parlour car. X: scrapped before 1948. 12: twelve-wheeled.

(See end for names of cars not noted but believed to have been running.)

Albatross (1897) A K X L
Albert Victor (1888) B P X
Alberta (1908) B Bk X 12
Alicante (1912) A K
Anaconda (1921) A K
Argus (1924) A K
Aurelia (1924) A K
Aurora (1923) A Bk L

Barbara (1926) A K L
Belgravia (1908) B K X 12

Cadiz (1921) A P 12
Calais (1921) A P 12
Camilla (1926) A K
Carmen (1896) A K L X
Cassandra (1926) A K
Cecilia (1927) A K
Chloria (1928) A K
Clementina (1910) A K L
Constance (1896) A K X L
Coral (1921) A K L X
Corunna (1910) A K L
Cosmo Bonsor (1912) A K L
Cynthia (1925) A K

Daphne (1914) B K L
Devonshire (1900) B P X 12
Diana (1891) B P X
Dolphin (1891) A L P X
Dora (1897) B L P X
Dorothy (1897) B L P X
Duchess of Connaught (1893) B P X
Duchess of Fife (1890) B P X
Duchess of Norfolk (1906) B K X 12

Elmira (1921) A K L
Emerald (1910) A K L
Erminie (1921) A K L

Falcon (1891) A L P X
Figaro (1896) B L P X
Fingall (1924) A K
Flora (1923) A Bk L P
Florence (1910) A K L
Formosa (1921) A K L

Geraldine (1924) A K
Grosvenor (1908) B K 12

Hawthorn (1914) A K L
Hibernia (1914) A K L 12
Hilda (1897) A K L X

Iolanthe (1923) B K

Juno (1923) A Bk L P

Latona (1926) A K
Leghorn (1910) A L P
Leona (1928) A P

Mabel (1896) A L P X
Madeline (1926) A K
Maid of Kent (1921) A K L
Majestic (1899) B P X 12
Malaga (1921) A K L 12
Marjorie (1924) A K
Medusa (1924) A K
Mimosa (1914) A K L
Monaco (1921) A K 12
Montana (1923) A Bk P

Neptune (1921) A K L 12
Niobe (1927) A P

Octavia (1927) B K

Padua (1920) A L P 12
Palermo (1910) B P
Palmyra (1921) A K L 12
Pauline (1924) A K
Pavilion (1893) B P X
Plato (1927) A K
Pomona (1926) A K
Portia (1920) A K L 12
Prince (1888) B P X
Princess Ena (1906) B K X 12
Princess Margaret (1890) B P X

Rainbow I(1927) B K X
Regina (1910) A K L
Rosalind (1921) A K 12
Rosemary (1923) A P
Ruby (1914) A K L

Sapphire (1910) A L P
Sappho (1924) A K
Savona (1910) A P L
Scotia (1914) A L P 12
Seville (1912) B K
Sorrento (1910) A P
Stella (1896) A L P X
Sunbeam (1921) A P 12
Sylvia (1921) A P 12

Theodora (1926) A K
Thistle (1897) A K L X
Topaz (1914) A L P
Tulip (1897) A L P X

Valencia (1910) A K
Venus (1897) A L P X
Verona (1908) B B Bk P X 12
Viking (1924) B K
Vivienne (1911) B P X 12

Waldemar (1897) B P X 12

Zenobia (1928) A K

Cars believed to have been on SR lines at the time but not noted.

Adrian (1928) K (3)
Bessborough (1908) P 12 (1)
Cleopatra (1908) P 12 (1)
Duke of Albany (1890) K (2)
Empress (1890) K (2)
Fortuna (1923) K (5)
Glencoe (1914) P 12 (5)
Ibis (1928) K (3)
Irene (1923) K (5)

Lydia (1928) K (3)
Milan (1921) K 12 (5)
Minerva (1927) P (4)
Myrtle (1911) K 12 (5)
Orpheus (1914) K 12 (5)
Pearl (1928) K (3)
Princess Helen (1908)12 (5)
Princess Mary (1893) K (2)
Princess Patricia (1906) K 12 (2

Notes: (1) 1908 'Belle' cars probably only being used on race trains.
        (2) Possibly stored as scrapped soon after.
        (3) Returned from Italy but not yet in service.
        (4) Probably on LNER at the time.
        (5) No explanation; just missed?

Only three cars on SR lines disappeared before 1927; *Mars* (1875) sold 1884; *Beatrice* (ex-MR *Globe* 1877) withdrawn 1918; *Maud* (ex-MR *Ceres* 1877) destroyed 1899.

Third class cars noted (all on former LBSC)

1	ex-*Jupiter* (1875), 3rd from 1915.
2	ex-*Victoria* (1876), 3rd from 1918?
5-7	*New* in 1917, 12w.
9	ex-*The Queen* (1890), 3rd from 1920.
10	ex-*Her Majesty* (1895), 3rd from 1922.
11-16	rebuilt from LNWR ambulance cars 1921.
17	new in 1923, 12w., ex-No. 50.
20	rebuilt from GWR ambulance car 1922.
22-26	rebuilt from L&YR ambulance cars 1922.
31-36	new in 1926.

All except 22/4/5/6 and 34-6 were kitchen cars; 25 and 26 were brake cars.

Regarding third-class cars not noted: No. 3 ex-*Alexandra* (1877) and No. 4 ex-*Albert Edward* (1877) may have been withdrawn. No. 8 was a rebuilt LNWR ambulance car. No. 18 ex-*Prince Regent* (1893) and No. 21, a rebuilt GWR ambulance car, are said to have been working elsewhere as second class cars. Nos. 19 and 17 appear to be numbers left blank by the withdrawal of some old demoted first class cars, and filled by renumbering two Clayton 12-wheelers on the LNER Scottish service, cars 51 and 50, to 19 and 17; 19 may not yet have been in service. With regard to Nos. 27-30, the information is not satisfactory. No. 27: sifting conflicting evidence, it seems likely it was built in 1923, then renumbered 80 (not on SR) and reverted to 27 when a new 80 was built in 1928. No information has been found on Nos. 28/9. No. 30 was a converted GWR ambulance car, possibly away at the time as a second class car.

In the early 1920s 'everyone who was anyone' had to take much of their pleasure in Paris, and they needed a luxury train to the short-sea-crossing ports. The Southern Railway was aware of this, but had inherited from the SE&CR little suitable stock; a train of old carriages with red Pullmans mixed in was not very grand. So the Pullman Company persuaded the SR to put on an all-Pullman train in the cream livery; this first ran on 17th November, 1924, and was usually referred to as the 'White Pullman' or the 'Dover Pullman Continental Express'. In the season the train was made up to nine Pullmans, one first class brake, two six-wheeled flat wagons for the customs-sealed baggage boxes, and two vans. This totalled around 450 tons, depending which cars were used, and required double-heading until 1926, by when the bridges on the ex-SER main line had been strengthened to take a 'Lord Nelson' or 'King Arthur' 4-6-0. Then in 1926 Pullman got the Nord Railway of France to put on a similar train from Calais to Paris, and dubbed it the 'Fleche d'Or' or 'Golden Arrow'; under this name the Dover train also ran from 1929, the 10.45 am from Victoria. From then the baggage cars mostly went down with the following 11 am, which took third class passengers but had four first class Pullmans. Both trains were often up to or over weight; for down trains the start was the hardest part and they were banked out towards Grosvenor Bridge by a 'T' class 0-6-0T puffing furiously. Often reliefs were also run, calling on the stock of red Pullmans.

This race special for Tattenham Corner in 1924 is made up from six former SER 'American Cars' with a 1910-1913 Pullman at each end, all in red livery. The 'N' class 2-6-0 has an experimental type of chimney.   *Lens of Sutton*

Two 'R' class 0-6-0Ts work hard to lift a Pullman train up the incline from Folkestone Harbour. Two or possibly three of the same type will be assisting at the rear; in August 1925 the cars are still in red livery.   *F. Foote*

The new Pullmans for this service were, firstly, four guard/parlour cars *Aurora, Flora, Juno* and *Montana,* the first three being outshopped in the old lake livery. Then there were kitchen cars *Argus, Geraldine, Marjorie, Sappho, Viking, Medusa, Pauline, Aurelia* and *Fingall.*

The 'Golden Arrow' was all-Pullman until 1932, when some ordinary carriages were added. Its success declined in the 'slump' years and at times it was reduced to four Pullmans. However, the Southern still regarded it as a prestige train and in 1938 provided refurbished coaches for it, in light olive green, to run with four 'renovated' Pullmans. The re-launch of this train after the War is described later. After the strengthening of the SER line to Dover, the former LCDR line was dealt with, and relief 'Continentals' often took this route. Some odd ones were seen, including a 'King Arthur' with two Pullmans and a van - an easy trip for the fireman.

All-Pullman trains were run for VIPs, such as a visit from the King of the Belgians in 1936; one was occasionally also laid on for the P&O Lines as the first leg of a journey to Marseilles for a liner cruise starting there.

In 1929 in preparation for Derby Day, a Pullman was tried working between two electric sets, the control cables passing through the car, but it was not in public use.

In 1924, following completion of the unscrambling of the SER/LCD competitive lines in the Margate and Ramsgate areas, a new service of London-Margate-Broadstairs-Ramsgate expresses was put on - sometimes called the Granville Expresses after some early special trains run for the Granville Hotel at Ramsgate. For this eight sets of new carriages were built, containing some fitted with adaptors for mating with Pullmans, and each set contained one first class Pullman car. At the same time a train was put on from Victoria to Dover via Maidstone East which included a first class Pullman. In 1926 six new first class cars were delivered for the Hastings service (via Tonbridge) of the restricted width necessitated by tunnels. These were: *Camilla, Latona, Madeline, Pomona, Theodora,* and *Barbara.* They worked singly, and from about 1933 became composites. Other new cars which came to the Eastern Section in 1927/8 were: *Cassandra, Plato, Cecilia, Chloria, Zenobia, Niobe* and *Leona.* They were needed, as the six former 'Hastings Car Train' cars had to be withdrawn at this time; one (*Carmen*) had in fact been destroyed in the 1927 Sevenoaks smash when a 'River' class 2-6-4T rolled off the track. The eight former 'Folkestone Car Train' cars went in 1930: they had been on excursion work and never bore the umber and cream livery.

The multiplicity of alternative routes to the coast remaining from the SER/LCD rivalry meant that Pullmans appeared at times in some odd places, especially after the bridges on the LCD line had been strengthened. In 1937 the 2.55 pm from Ramsgate ran via Catford Bridge and actually stopped there, also at Lewisham, before taking the Nunhead Loop to Victoria. Two trains were running with Pullmans from Dover via Canterbury, allowing stations such as Shepherdswell to have a Pullman train stopping there. Cars were also appearing more and more on 'foreign' excursions; one from Tunbridge Wells to Bourneville had a Pullman, and a Hastings line car was noted at Bolton on a football train.

There are eleven Pullmans on this down 'Southern Belle' in 1929, three of them old American cars; the 'King Arthur' class of 4-6-0 used six-wheeled tenders on the Brighton run.   *R.W. Airy*

Brake car 40 and parlour 84 lead the inaugural trip on the 'Bournemouth Belle' leaving Waterloo on 5th July, 1931.   *H.G. Tidey*

In October 1936 the 'Night Ferry' started running from Victoria to Paris and Brussels, most of the train crossing the Channel on new train-ferry vessels. Originally the formation was: five Wagons-Lits sleeping cars, three carriages, a Pullman and a van. The Pullman was taken off for a while, but later two Pullmans were included. The Wagon-Lits cars ran in blue livery of the Compagnie International des Wagons-Lits, whose connection with the Pullman Car Co. was more obvious across the channel. The links between the Pullman Company and the Compagnie International des Wagons-Lits were too complex for full understanding; financial connections were well hidden, and it was customary in this country for Pullman people to deny any connection with CIWL. This confused many, as some cars on the other side of the Channel, undeniably CIWL property, also carried the words 'Pullman Car'.

This train, and the growing cross-channel air services, brought a steady decline in the number and loadings of Continental Expresses, and thus the number of Pullman cars on these trains, which for 25 years had seen the matching of 'beautiful people' to 'beautiful Pullmans' as nowhere else.

The only event of note in the early years on the former LBSC line was the announcement that an 'entirely new' 'Southern Belle' train would run as from 1st January, 1925. The splendid 1908 train had only seen some 13 years of service, due to the War, but perhaps its weight and low seating capacity caused the decision to take it off. The Southern Railway often used the word 'new' merely to mean 'different' and this was certainly the case here. The third class cars were some of those rebuilt in 1921 from former ambulance cars; the first class cars, in so far as they can be traced, seem to have been some post-war ones originally intended for the LNER or the Eastern Section of the SR, including *Iolanthe*, *Viking* and *Rosamund*. Although the Section had two third class 'end-cars' (Nos. 25/26) they do not seem to have been used, as photographs show the train with bogie brake vans at each end at first. The steam 'Belle' had only another seven years to run, and during this period it was very variable in format: the Sunday first-class-only train had to lean heavily on the old American cars. With an electric 'Belle' already a gleam in the eyes of certain parties at Waterloo, there was naturally no incentive to make much of the steam version. The 1908 12-wheelers were also used to help out - two of their 1911 look-alikes (*Myrtle* and *Vivienne*) were on the train in 1931, by which time there were seven thirds and only three firsts on the weekday train.

One prestige train which had not included a Pullman in recent years was the 'City Limited', the 8.48 am from Brighton and 5 pm from London Bridge. In 1925 an entirely new train of Eastleigh-built stock was provided for this, but still no Pullman. However, in February 1926 one first was taken out and the car *Princess Patricia* put in. It is perhaps worth recording here that cars seldom stayed long on one stint; on this duty *Grosvenor* appeared later in 1926, followed at roughly yearly intervals by *Iolanthe*, *Regina*, *Anaconda* and *Coral*. Some regular travellers may have formed an affection for an individual car, but if they did so the Pullman Company did not respond. Perhaps only railwayists noted names; a correspondent in the *Railway Magazine* in 1954 recalled that the Pullman in the London Bridge portion of the 5 pm from Brighton 50 years earlier 'was usually *Jupiter*' - at least someone remembered them.

A 12-wheeled kitchen car is the second one on this double-headed Epsom Downs race special about 1934; the combination of an ex-LBSC 'E5' 0-6-2T and an ex-SECR 'H' class 0-4-4T was unusual.   *Lens of Sutton*

The lights of the evening 'Brighton Belle' made a welcoming sight at Victoria for tired commuters; set 2051 is seen here early in 1933.   *Author*

In 1926 the new 'King Arthur' class 4-6-0 was introduced to the Brighton fast trains, though the Atlantics and Baltic Tanks also continued on the rosters up to the last days.   From contemporary records it seems that all were equally capable. In June 1931 an Atlantic took the 'City Limited' down in 56½ minutes net; an 'Arthur' with the same 400-ton load equalled this time from Victoria; and a 4-6-4T with 430 tons had a 58½ minutes net time in the up direction.

The electric 'Southern Belle', which began running on 1st January, 1933, represented a brave move, but perhaps an unnecessary risk, for the quick turn-around that was the main advantage of multiple-units was not really necessary for this duty. The question was: could a 62-ton motored car, of which there was one at each end of the three five-car 'Belle' sets, provide the sort of comfortable running that Pullman passengers expected? On the opening run, a group of madrigal ladies strolled along the train to show how quiet and smooth it was. In the opinion of the author, who was a passenger, the test failed - and they could only stroll half-way down each way as there was no connection between sets. However, these sets remained in use for 40 years and achieved affection from regular travellers, who perhaps left the end cars to day-trippers. At a ceremony in Brighton on 29th June, 1934, the train was renamed 'The Brighton Belle'. Incidentally, the original name was inspired by W.S. Forbes of the LBSC, nephew of the famous J.S. Forbes of the LCDR. The 'Belle' sets were originally numbered 2051-3, and named cars were: (2051) *Hazel* and *Doris*, (2052) *Vera* and *Audrey*, (2053) *Mona* and *Gwen*. The third class cars as usual carried only numbers, 85-93.

Also on 1st January, 1933 six-coach emus took over the express working to Brighton. These sets included a composite Pullman in each. There were twenty 6-PUL sets (2001-20), and three 6-CIT sets (2041-3) with initially more first class accommodation, as was required for the 'City Limited'. After a short time one set was swapped for a West Worthing Pullman working, and the train ran as 6-PUL+6-CIT. For the first two years almost all Brighton expresses in peak hours had two Pullmans, though as there were no corridors through motor coaches, passengers could not make contact with each other. From 1935 when 17 more six-car sets were built for the Eastbourne and Hastings line, with pantry cars, it became customary for trains to be 6-PUL+6-PAN on both Brighton and Hastings lines.

The composite cars in the 6-PUL and 6-CIT sets all had names, as follows:

2001	*Anne*			2011	*Naomi*
2002	*Rita*			2012	*Bertha*
2003	*Grace*			2013	*Brenda*
2004	*Elinor*			2014	*Enid*
2005	*Ida*			2015	*Joyce*
2006	*Rose*			2016	*Iris*
2007	*Violet*			2017	*Ruth*
2008	*Lorna*			2018	*May*
2009	*Alice*			2019	*Peggy*
2010	*Daisy*			2020	*Clara*
2041	*Gwladys*	2042	*Olive*	2043	*Ethel*

Set numbers were altered to 3XXX in 1937.

After the Brighton electrification, work was found for the displaced Pullman cars partly on the Eastbourne and Bognor trains; after the former line was also electrified there were even more spare. However, business in Pullman Specials was good; not only race specials, but also royals and semi-royals, and trips to important business and State events. The 1935 Derby Day saw two all-Pullmans specials on the Epsom Downs line, both double-headed with two tank engines, and at least two more to Tattenham Corner in charge of 'N' class 2-6-0s. On occasion SR Pullmans were lent to the LNER for Newmarket race specials. As there were seldom any 'end-cars' available for these specials, something had to be provided for the guard. The Central Section had three unusual bogie brakes, two with clerestory roofs (Nos. 928/9) and one of 'Balloon' outline (No. 909) and these were most often used, perhaps because they gave a better impression than the flat-roofed varieties.

Despite all this, however, Pullmans were being scrapped, and in some cases the bodies sold for as little as £50. One such on Bishopstone beach had noble company, an equerries' saloon from the LBSC Royal Train and a first from the old 'City Limited'. In the period 1929-32 forty-eight cars were taken out of service on the SR, including all but two of the pre-1908 ones, and all the converted SER American cars. Official figures early in 1933 gave the Pullman Co. as having 112 first class cars, 40 composites, 73 thirds, and 32 dining cars (mostly on the LMS). As all the cars on the LMS would be sold to that railway in 1933, it is clear that the peak figure for Pullmans in traffic must have been passed some time during 1932, the actual date depending on the inter-action of withdrawals with the commissioning of new electric cars. The number schedule begun in 1915, including all cars in service at that date and later, had reached 300 by 1933; only one non-SR car had been withdrawn.

In 1935 the Pullman Company took a hard look at its future requirements on the Southern Railway. The fleet was now reasonably modern; almost all the American cars went in a sweep in 1932, and the few left then were now gone. There were the old 1908 'Belle' cars, heavy 12-wheelers. Mr G.H. Griffith, general manager, announced 'no further use is in prospect for them'. So they all went except one, *Grosvenor*, which was converted into a bar car, as was *Myrtle*, one of the 1911 12-wheelers. Although earlier Pullmans had had small 'bars', the new conception was for a long bar with seats, and a few more at the end of the car. It was for passengers to move in and out of; both cars were seen on the Newhaven boat trains and were popular. A few old cars were painted all-over umber and put on to cheap excursion trains, but details of their use are scarce. The Bognor and Portsmouth line was of course still finding employment for Pullmans, but electrification was in progress and was completed by 1938. The new trains were to have restaurant or pantry cars, not Pullmans; by 3rd July, 1938 there were no Pullmans in regular steam-hauled service anywhere on the Central Section.

However, the Pullman Co. could congratulate itself on one score. The King and Queen had made little use of the Southern Railway Royal Train of late, and in fact in 1939 it was demoted to work the Brookwood Necropolis service. For some years Pullmans had been used instead, and the frequent press photographs of royal personages stepping from Pullman cars at Platform 2 at

Victoria helped to keep up the Pullman image. The company never had an official 'Royal Saloon' though no doubt care was taken in choosing the stock, which usually ran to four cars, to accommodate the entourage. For example, when Their Majesties paid a state visit to France in July 1938, *Minerva* was used; on their return from their Canadian tour in June 1939, *Niobe* was the Royal Saloon.

Pullman cars returned to the former LSWR in January 1931, when some cars were put on the Ocean Liner Expresses to Southampton, usually two to four per train. These were mainly cars which had just had a very short term with the Great Western Railway: *Evadne, Loraine, Ione, Joan, Juana, Eunice,* and *Zena;* also six former 'Queen of Scots' cars.

On 5th July, 1931 came the inaugural journey of the 'Bournemouth Belle', serving Bournemouth and for a time Weymouth. The train was summer-only on weekdays from 1931 to 1936, though it ran on Sundays in winter. After the first summer season, the Weymouth portion was discontinued. This had comprised five coaches from the 10-car train, taken off at Central before the remainder went on to Bournemouth West. As usual, it was announced as an entirely new train, but in fact only four cars were new. The formation was: third class cars 40, 84, 82, 60, first class *Flora, Montana, Aurelia,* third class 81, 83, 41. Only cars 81-4 were new, the rest being of 1920-5 build. The handsome end-cars, Nos. 40/41, had originally been built for the Great Eastern Railway in 1920, but only four years later were rebuilt as brakes for the Great Northern section of the LNER. The brake and luggage compartments measured 22 ft. Two first class cars, *Ansonia* and *Arcadia,* with the same history, which later came to the SR as thirds 94/5, had 23 ft 8 in. luggage spaces. These long brake-ends, painted brown all over, made a break from tradition on the SR. The rolling doors were fitted during the 1924 rebuild.

The early stirrings of long-distance air transport also brought work for Pullmans in this area; special trains, usually of four cars, were run as required to Bournemouth for Hurn Airport, and Poole for the flying boats. The latter also worked for a time from Hythe (Hants), the Empire Flying Boat Service, and passengers were ferried across Southampton Water using Hythe Pier, to and from a single Pullman and van, joined up with a boat train within the Docks.

Under the dynamic control of the Southern Railway, Southampton increased its traffic enormously, and Ocean Liner Expresses and Pullman Specials proliferated. An observer in 1932 noted 17 up Ocean Liner Expresses one day, 12 with Pullmans. Pullmans were also included in the Channel Islands boat trains, and on 15th August, 1936 one of them, *Rainbow,* caught fire *en route* and had to be detached while burning at Micheldever. This was especially embarrassing since the following train was the 'Bournemouth Belle' loaded to 12 cars. Such a load could not be taken round the steeply-graded Alton line to avoid the fire, so it was run-round at Winchester, worked tender-first to Eastleigh, sent to Salisbury where it reversed, and arrived at Waterloo three hours late. No doubt the drinks profits for the day were high.

The down 'Bournemouth Belle' at Worting Junction on 31st August, 1934, hauled by 'Lord Nelson' class 4-6-0 No. 851.   *Author*

This Southampton boat train seen at Basingstoke includes three Pullman cars, made available by the demise of the GWR's 'Torquay Pullman', seen on 15th May, 1937.   *Author*

Table Two - Down Pullman trains in the 1931 winter timetable (weekdays)

Central Section

		Class of Pullman
8.50 am	Victoria-Portsmouth	3rd
9.05	Victoria-Brighton	1st & 3rd
10.00	Victoria-Newhaven	1st (two)
10.05	Victoria-Brighton	1st & 3rd
11.05	Victoria-Brighton	1st & 3rd. All Pullman
11.15	Victoria- Eastbourne	1st & 3rd
12.05 pm	Victoria-Brighton	1st & 3rd
12.35	Victoria-Brighton SO	1st & 3rd
1.00	London Bridge-Brighton SO	1st & 3rd
1.10	Victoria-Brighton SO	1st & 3rd
1.48	London Bridge-Eastbourne SO	1st
2.05	Victoria-Brighton	1st & 3rd
3.05	Victoria-Brighton	1st & 3rd. All Pullman
3.15	Victoria-Eastbourne	1st & 3rd
3.20	Victoria-Bognor	1st & 3rd
3.35	Victoria-Brighton	1st & 3rd
3.35	Victoria-W. Worthing	3rd
4.00	London Bridge-Brighton	3rd
4.05	London Bridge-Eastbourne	1st
4.35	Victoria-Brighton	1st & 3rd
5.00	London Bridge-Brighton SX	1st
5.05	London Bridge-Eastbourne SX	1st
5.08	London Bridge-W. Worthing SX	1st
5.20	Victoria- Eastbourne	1st & 3rd
5.35	Victoria-Brighton	1st & 3rd
5.40	Victoria-W. Worthing	1st & 3rd
6.00	London Bridge-Brighton	3rd
6.05	Victoria-Brighton SX	1st & 3rd
7.05	Victoria-Brighton	1st & 3rd
8.05	Victoria-Brighton	1st & 3rd
8.20	Victoria-Newhaven	1st (two)
10.05	Victoria-Brighton	1st & 3rd
11.05	Victoria-Brighton	1st & 3rd
12.05	Victoria-Brighton	1st & 3rd

Eastern Section

Former SER main line: 1st class Pullman:

11.30 am	Ramsgate SO	All from Charing Cross except 5.00 pm, from Cannon Street.
12.55 pm	Margate SO	
1.15	Ramsgate SX	
4. 15	Ramsgate	
5.0	Ramsgate	
5.15	Ramsgate SO	
7. 15	Margate	

Hastings line: 1st class Pullman, from Charing Cross: on 10.40 am, 12.25, 3.20, 7.20 pm; from Cannon Street, 1.04 (SO), 5.04, 6.00 pm.

Former LC&D main line to Ramsgate: first class Pullman on following trains from Victoria: 8.55,10.34 (SO), 11.25 (SO) am, 1.10 (SO), 3.10 (SO), 3.15 (SX), 6.08 (SX), 7.00, 9.00 pm. From Cannon Street, 1.12 (SO), 5.06 (SX), 5.16 (SO), 5.46 (SX), 6.08 (SX) pm.

Continental trains, all from Victoria: Folkestone-Boulogne, 9.00, 10.00 am, 2 pm; Dover-Calais, 11.00 (all-Pullman), 11.15 am, 4.00 pm. Ostend served by 10.00 am and 2.00 pm. All trains advertised as 1st or 1st/2nd only, except 4.00 pm which served 3rd class for destinations outside France. It does not appear that any Pullmans other than 1st class were used.

Western Section

9.00 pm   Waterloo-Southampton-Havre: Timetable implies a Pullman.

It is worth while looking also at the Sunday service on the Brighton main line, as this was a field-day for Pullmans, especially 3rd class ones. The 'Southern Belle' was first-class-only all day, and ran down at 11.05 am, with two return trains from Brighton at 5.00 pm and 7.05. The 'Pullman Limited' which was all-Pullman and third class only, went down at 9.45 am and returned from Brighton at 6.35 pm. In addition there was an all-Pullman two-class train, not named, which left Victoria at 11.35 am and returned from Brighton at 4.35 pm. The 'Eastbourne Sunday Pullman', 1st and 3rd, left Victoria at 10.45 am and left Eastbourne (not all-Pullman) at 6.20 pm. With four all-Pullman trains leaving Victoria in under two hours in winter-time, the popularity of the cars could not be doubted - however, it must have called for some shunting on Saturday. It must be remembered that there were also two boat trains with Pullmans each way, and other trains to Worthing, Brighton and Eastbourne with the usual quota of two cars. The morning train to Portsmouth which included only a third class Pullman also ran on Sundays, but via Dorking instead of via Crawley and took the opportunity of stopping at Dorking North, surely the only Pullman train to serve this station .

Southern Railway - The War and After

In September 1939 all Pullmans were locked or withdrawn in the first panic of War. The 'Bournemouth Belle' suffered the indignity of being pushed into Tolworth goods sidings. However, on 1st January, 1940 new orders took effect and some were restored; on 27th March, 1940 a Pullman was restored on five Hastings trains in each direction. The *Railway Magazine* reported that by May 1940 there were 36 Pullmans working on the Central Section and 24 on the Eastern; after the fall of France the pattern changed and in May 1941 there were 48 on the Central and 22 on the Eastern. One 'Brighton Belle' set was running usually attached to a 6-PUL set; however, after set 3052 had been heavily damaged by bombs near Victoria on 9th October, 1940, all the three sets were withdrawn. On 22nd May, 1942 all Pullmans were finally withdrawn, except those on War service, and the 6-PUL sets became five-coach.

Some cars were made use of; one case was the special train which ran each night from the north-west end of Victoria station, near the then BOAC terminal building, to Bournemouth for Hurn airfield and Poole for the flying boats. The passengers were mostly in the VIP category; when noted in 1945 the train comprised only two Pullmans, a first class carriage and a van.

Some major damage was done when on 25th May, 1943 bombs dropped on the Pullman train-shed at Preston Park. Third class cars 12, 20 and 40 were destroyed and others damaged; another bomb on Brighton a month later damaged a further nine cars.

While the War was on not much notice was taken of the former Pullmans now running in various guises. From 1942 some were on hire to NAAFI and had their own number series; a few seem to have been semi-static. As the War ended 10 NAAFI cars were allocated to five BAOR leave trains; these were still running as single cars into 1947. All seem to have been green, although some brown cars were also seen on other jobs. One person who did take some notes in 1944, Mr R.C. Riley, has kindly allowed these to be used here; of course they only take in a proportion of the Pullmans either in use or stored at conveniently quiet locations.

Crystal Palace High Level, 22nd January, 1944: 'Belle' set 3052 tarpaulin-covered, badly shrapnel-pitted.
Horsted Keynes, 28th February, 1944: *Sylvia, Cadiz, Sunbeam, Padua.*
Polegate, April 1944: *Topaz, Glencoe, Aurora.*
Eardley Road Sidings, 17th May, 1944: in original livery, *Pearl, Sylvia, Grosvenor, Myrtle*; in khaki, *Sappho, Monaco, Anaconda.*
Aldershot, 19th May, 1944: Car No. 19, grey (seen next month at Eardley).
Burgess Hill, 24th June, 1944: *Mimosa, Hawthorn, Florence, Madeline,* two more.
Coulsdon North, 24th June, 1944: nine cars from 6-PUL sets: *Olive, May, Bertha, Brenda, Rose, Grace, Enid, Gwladys, Daisy.*
Preston Park, March-June 1944: *Fingall,* Car 24, *Leona, Clara, Iris, Aurora, Aurelia, Myrtle, Grosvenor.*
Tonbridge, August 1944: *Savona.*
Sidley, August 1944: Car *31, Malaga, Neptune, Orpheus, Hibernia.*
Polegate, October 1944; *Eunice, Evadne, Zena, Juana, Lucille, Loraine, Ursula, Leona.*

Cars were certainly moving around, though probably mainly for painting and preserving; no cars had been varnished since the beginning of the War, and those that showed signs of deterioration were treated with red or grey lead oxide paint.

When the War ended a lot of movement began; the LNER cars had been stored on the SR, and cars of both railways did not all return whence they came, some SR cars going on to the 'Queen of Scots' and 'Tyne-Tees', and some LNER cars on to the 'Golden Arrow', and so on. The electric cars, when dragged out of store, did not all return to their original sets.

Thoughts of re-starting Pullman services were quick to arise; as early as October 1945 a 10-car all-Pullman train was noted behind 'Merchant Navy' Pacific No. 21C2 on a proving trip to Dover, and the same train was seen early in 1946 behind electric locomotive No. CC2 doing a twice-daily run to Brighton, not in public service. One of the 'Belle' sets was working from 24th April, 1946, coupled either to a 4-COR or 6-PUL set; however, repairs on the bomb-damaged set 3052 were now being done and the train was fully restored on 6th October, 1947. Pullmans were replaced in the 6-PUL sets as from early May 1946.

The 'Devon Belle', which had a portion for Plymouth dropped off at Exeter, was a heavy train of 13 or 14 cars, the end one being an observation saloon. The locomotive here is 'Merchant Navy' class No. 21C7 *Aberdeen Commonwealth*.   *Lens of Sutton*

The newly-restored 'Golden Arrow' Pullman train near Bickley in August 1946, with 'West Country' Pacific No. 21C130; it is on the spur line enabling trains from Victoria to join the ex-SER main line.   *Author*

On the Hastings (former SECR) line Pullmans were also restored, but only three cars, and these were de-classed and lost their names, simply carrying 'Restaurant Car' on the sides. No supplement was charged. The three cars were *Barbara*, *Madeline* and *Pomona*; their schedule numbers (182, 183, 185) were also carried on the sides. The other three former Hastings line cars were transferred to work on Southampton Boat Trains.

In view of the enormous difficulty in procuring any supplies such as paint or timber, the Pullman Company did very well to restore services - and start new ones - as soon as they did. There were few observers with the opportunity to cover developments as they unfolded; however, Mr R.C. Riley was again able to take some interesting notes (all 1946):

> 13th September, cars 32 and 33 noted newly painted in Brighton carriage sidings (these were later on the 'Devon Belle').
>
> 28th September, in South Croydon sidings (the old terminal station platforms): *Scotia* (brown), *Topaz*, Car No. 11, *Aurelia*, Car. No. 8 (grey), Car No. 13 (green), Car No. 30, *Leghorn*, *Elmira*, *Erminie*.
>
> 30th September, at Stewarts Lane: Car No. 1 (the second, *ex-Emerald*) green livery.
>
> October, in Lancing Works; *Grosvenor*, *Myrtle*, *Curnillu*, *Veru*, *Ruby*, *Padua*, *Ibis*, *Latona*, *Fingall* (later on the 'Tyne-Tees').
>
> 25th October, at Preston Park: *Myrtle* with roof cut down to allow working over Eastern Section (this was one of the 13 ft high cars).
>
> 27th December, Preston Park: *Cynthia*, *Vera*, *Regina*, *Loraine* (brown), *Eunice*, *Lucille*. At Burgess Hill: *Formosa*, *Malaga*. At Hove: Car No. 9, *Palmyra*.

The work of overcoming wartime depredations and complications went on; a visit to Preston Park on 14th February, 1947 revealed, amongst others, *Zena* in green livery, *Princess Elizabeth* in red lead, and Car No. 26 as LNER 489.

The 'Golden Arrow' was restored from 15th April, 1946. There had been a run for the press on the 13th, rather marred by the fact that the new 'Trianon Bar' Car, former 3rd class car No. 5 entirely rebuilt, ran hot on the way down and had to be taken off; the other cars were *Lady Dalziel* (brake), *Adrian*, *Sappho*, *Niobe*, *Onyx*, *Cecilia*, and 2nd class cars 194 (ex-36) and 154 (ex-*Flora*, brake). The former car *Diamond* was hastily got up as a 'Trianon Bar' for the 15th, but No. 5 returned in July and served until 1951 when the new 'Arrow' stock appeared. (*Diamond* was possibly the only car to serve on all four Regions of BR; she was renamed 'One Hundred Bar' and then 'New Century Bar' for the Ostend boat trains, then having a centenary, and in 1955 'Daffodil Bar' for the WR South Wales Pullman, later going on to both Eastern and London Midland under various guises.) The new 'Golden Arrow' was decked out with gold arrows and 'Golden Arrow' and 'Fleche D'Or' on both engine and Pullmans.

The 'Bournemouth Belle' was restored on 7th October, 1946. It was considered that its future lay mainly with third class passengers, and it only had four first class Pullmans (*Philomel*, *Ibis*, *Rosemary* and *Lydia*); the third class cars were 17, 19 and 94-99; these last were six former first class cars, two from the LNER. This made a 12-car train, but at slack times two or four cars were taken out.

A new all-Pullman train began running on 20th June, 1947, the 'Devon Belle', from Waterloo to Ilfracombe, with initially a Plymouth portion dropped at

One of many cars to suffer considerable alteration, third class No. 11 was converted by Clayton from an LNWR hospital coach in 1921, and rebuilt as a brake car at Preston Park in 1949, having been a bar car since 1937.

Lens of Sutton

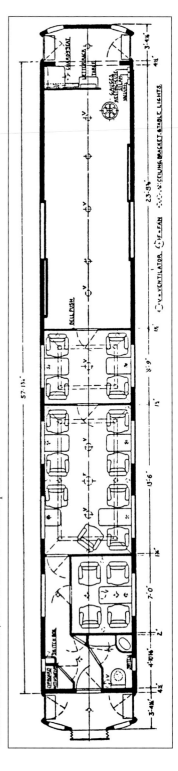

Plan of 12-wheeled car *Arcadia*, as rebuilt in 1924 from the 1920 parlour car, with 23 ft 8 in. guard and luggage space; in 1935 became third class No. 95; worked on LNER and SR; 63 ft 10 in. over vestibule plates.

Exeter. This ran on summer weekends, Friday to Monday, and from 1948, Tuesdays and Thursdays also. The two trains providing the service both had observation cars, made out of old third class cars, which required turning and running round at termini; another unusual feature was that for the first few years the train did not stop at Salisbury, engines being changed at Wilton. As this train spent most of its life under BR, it will be dealt with in the next section.

In post-war conditions more third class cars would be needed; some were created instantly by screwing number boards over names. Demotions included four of the six cars rebuilt in 1921 from LNWR ambulances; *Anaconda, Erminie, Elmira,* and *Maid of Kent (I)* became third class Nos. 132,133,135,137. There were no numbers 134 or 136, because *Coral,* which would have had the first number, was not demoted, and *Formosa,* which would have been 136, was renamed *Maid of Kent* (II) for the 'Thanet Belle'. There was also a call for more 'end cars' and several were so rebuilt at Preston Park.

This was a time when many Pullman-watchers became confused over numbering. Although the original 'third class' series retained its low numbers, new conversions to third class took their higher 'schedule' numbers, though illogically when cars 11, 15 and 16 were converted to brakes they kept their old numbers, as did 13 and 14 when made into observation cars. The highest numbers in the old third class series were 105-7 for some 'Yorkshire Pullman' cars in 1946. Those quoted above, 132/3/5/7, were *schedule* numbers used as third class numbers. A good example of how confusion could arise is provided by cars 94-99. Nos. 94/5 (ex-*Ansonia* and *Arcadia*) did not take their schedule numbers, which were 108/9, when converted to third class: however, cars 96-99 *did* take their schedule numbers. Schedule 94 and 95 (*Neptune* and *Sunbeam*) stayed first class.

Under British Railways

It might have been expected that the private Pullman Car company would be ground into British Transport Commission anonymity after Nationalisation, but this was not so. In fact in many ways this was to be the period of the most use of Pullmans. In 1948, however, the fact had to be faced that no new cars had been built for 16 years; it was fortunate that few of the cars made redundant by the electrification programme had in fact been scrapped. One of the first new Pullman trains, the Sunday 'Eastbourne Pullman Limited' needed none since it used a spare 'Brighton Belle' set. This first ran on 31st May, 1948, and on the same day the 'Thanet Belle' (later renamed 'Kentish Belle') was put on between Victoria and Ramsgate. This had eight third class cars and only two first class. It was made up from old cars - but there was no shame in that. The present Queen's honeymoon train used the Pullmans *Rosemary* and *Rosamund,* so 20-year-old cars were adequate for her. As with a woman, one did not ask a Pullman car her age.

The launching of the 'Devon Belle' has been mentioned in the last chapter. There were two trains of 12 cars each, and each was tailed by an observation car. These cars, Nos. 13 and 14, were former third class parlour cars, rebuilds from

The 'Thanet Belle' featured a specially designed tailboard as well as a headboard; the down working is seen here near Birchington. *J.C. Flemens*

The Clayton car *Formosa* was renamed *Maid of Kent* to run on the 'Thanet Belle', in 1948 it is seen here at Preston Park in 1959. The original *Maid of Kent* became third class No. 137 at the same time. *J.H.W. Kent*

Car No. 14 was built in 1921 for LBSC third class work, on the frame of an LNWR ambulance car, and was completely rebuilt to become one of the tail-cars of the two 'Devon Belle' trains. Seen here at Clapham Junction sidings waiting to be hauled to Waterloo for the down working.
Lens of Sutton

The 'Devon Belle' required some shunting to place the observation car, duly turned, at the rear. Here a 'W' class 2-6-4T is at Clapham Junction after sorting out for the down run.
Lens of Sutton

After the electrification of the ex-LBSC main lines there were Pullmans available for private trains; here third class car 99, former kitchen car *Padua* is at Brighton on an RCTS special hauled by a Marsh Atlantic in 1952.

The 'New Century Bar' car, formerly *Diamond*, at Clapham Junction in July 1954 after being taken off the Ostend trains to be remodelled as 'The Daffodil Bar' for the 'South Wales Pullman'.

H.C. Casserley

LNWR ambulance carriages. In their new form they had built-in bars, and 27 seats facing a sloping glazed end. A correspondent in the Press commented that these were made uncomfortable enough to deter any one passenger from staying too long. Fortunately, the excellent view of an 'N' class 2-6-0 banking the train up to Mortehoe summit was of interest only to railwayists - otherwise there would have been a mad scramble somewhere around Braunton. The front four cars in both directions were the Plymouth section, detached at Exeter. The formation just before Nationalisation had been: Plymouth portion, Cars 54, 33, *Argus*, Car 208; main train, *Princess Elizabeth, Rosamund, Geraldine*, Cars 34, 249, 32, 27, 13. Second train, Plymouth portion: Cars 55, 61, *Iolanthe*, Car 36; main train, *Minerva, Cynthia, Fingall*, Cars 35, 169, 60, 63, 14. A year later eight of these had changed; in summer 1948 the formations were: Train No. 1, Plymouth portion: Car 36, *Iolanthe*, Car 54; main train, *Princess Elizabeth, Ibis*, Cars 34, 33, 32, 27, 13. Train No. 2, Plymouth portion, Car 208, *Cynthia*, Car 55; main train, *Minerva, Penelope*, Cars 35, 61, 31, 65, 14.

This train was not a great success; from 1950 on the Plymouth portion was dropped, and in 1952 it was announced the train would not run; however, it was reprieved as a week-end only train until September 1954. By that time it was bearing witness to the continuing demoting of first class cars, since it included third class cars 161 (ex-*Fortuna*), 162 (ex-*Irene*), 166 (ex-*Geraldine*), 167 (ex-*Viking*), 171 (ex-*Pauline*), and 248 (ex-*Lady Dalziel*). Ilfracombe did in fact see one more Pullman train when, on 19th October, 1963, the *Flying Scotsman* arrived there with a Pullman Special.

During the week, and after the train's demise, the observation cars were in demand for special trains; from the operational point of view, it was better if these were round tours and called for no observation car turning. When in April 1951 part of the 'Devon Belle' was used for a visit to the Grain oil terminal, the whole train was turned on a triangle inside the complex; there were other triangles such as those at Branksome and Eastleigh which could come in useful. In 1961 the observation cars were used on the Inverness-Kyle of Lochalsh and Glasgow-Oban services, but No. 13 is now back in Devon still rolling happily after 70 years in various guises.

It was the preparations for the 1951 Festival of Britain which gave Pullman car construction a much-needed boost. It was considered that the influx of tourists for the event would justify new Pullman trains, which would also serve for the very many VIP specials expected. An order placed with Birmingham C&W in 1938, which had not been progressed, was restarted with some modifications to design, and the following new cars appeared in 1951: first class: parlour cars *Perseus, Cyanus* and *Hercules*, bar car *Pegasus*, kitchen cars *Aquila, Orion* and *Carina*: also second class car No. 303. Most of these were put on to a new 'Golden Arrow'. In addition, the 1927 first brake *Minerva* and second brake car 208 (formerly LNER *Leona*) were refurbished, as were former third class cars 34-6 of 1926; in 1952 two more new cars came from the Pullman works, *Phoenix* (on the frame of burnt *Rainbow*) and *Aries*. The new 'Golden Arrow' first ran on 11th June, 1951, the formation being: *Minerva, Aquila, Cygnus, Pegasus, Hercules, Orion, Perseus, Carina*, second class car No. 35, second class car No. 208. *Pegasus* contained a new 'Trianon Bar'. Not long after this the

The 'Golden Arrow' leaving Victoria in September 1956, hauled by a 'Britannia' class Pacific No. 70014; at this time the train always had a bogie utility van at its south end. Note the square end windows on the cars, replacing the former ovals. *Author*

The 10-car 'Brighton Belle' on Grosvenor Bridge in September 1956; set 3051 is leading; all four motor coaches were third class. *Author* train lost its down end 'end-car' and usually ran with a bogie utility van, or a four-wheel van plus baggage car; later still with a GUV at each end.

The new cars, which were built on LNER-type frames with 8 ft 6 in. double-bolster bogies, differed only from the old style in having square, instead of oval, small windows. They were used on many VIP specials, usually four-car, and perhaps the smartest ever seen, with the 'Merchant Navy' Pacific picked out in white on wheel rims and bosses, buffer faces, brake pipes, smoke deflector edges. Usually it carried an armorial device of the country concerned in a round panel over the smoke-box door.

For the 1951 season the 'Thanet Belle' was renamed 'Kentish Belle' and ran twice daily on weekdays, as it always had on Saturdays. During the 'Festival' period a portion of the train was detached at Faversham and worked to Canterbury. Soon after, this 'Belle' became a mixed train, and ceased to run on 14th September, 1958.

A development of 1952 was the naming of various Southampton Boat Trains, for instance 'The Cunarder' and 'The Statesman' (United States Lines), some workings being all-Pullman.

Motive power was of course changing; the 'Bournemouth Belle' was first diesel-hauled in October 1951, though still mainly steam, including oddly enough in May 1953 the ex-LNER 'V2' Pacifics, at a time when 'Merchant Navy' class engines were temporarily withdrawn. The easily-forgettable diesels Nos. 10201/2/3 were seen on the 'Bournemouth Belle' and the 'Golden Arrow', and electric locomotive No. 20001 on race specials to Epsom Downs. In 1953 all Pullman train headboards were re-designed, partly to make them easily transferable between engine classes; all had been designed to fit the Bulleid Pacific lamp-iron placings.

At the end of the last section the 1947 'Bournemouth Belle' was described. By the mid-1950s only four of those cars were still on it, Nos. 17 and 97-9; the first class cars were now *Topaz*, *Hibernia*, *Sunbeam*, and *Rosalind*; replacement thirds were Nos. 6, 47 and 303. This last car, a brake, was allotted its schedule number as its 'third class' number when built in 1952 - though in fact it ran as second class No. 303 for a time on the 'Golden Arrow'. In 1960 some more Eastern Region cars, displaced by new stock, came to the SR; by the time the 'Bournemouth Belle' died, on 9th July, 1967, three of them, *Ursula*, *Phyllis* and *Lucille* were on it, also *Aquila*, and seconds 34, 61, 64, 75, 76, all but one originally LNER. The 12-wheeled end-cars had gone, and there was a van at each end.

In 1964 Lord Beaulieu took on to his museum site a 'Schools' 4-4-0 and three Pullmans, exhibited as 'The Bournemouth Belle'; the cars were *Fingall*, *Agatha*, and Car No. 35, though it is not certain that *Agatha*, a 'Queen of Scots' car, had ever worked on the Southern. In 1972 the cars went to Haven Street, IoW, but later *Agatha* came back, for the VSOE (*see later*) and *Fingall* for the Bluebell Railway.

Now that much of the Pullman traffic was in Specials, they popped up in some strange places; in November 1954 a 'Royal' for the Emperor of Ethiopia from Portsmouth to Victoria went via Mitcham Junction; one for the Queen ran to Fort Brockhurst. Even the 'Brighton Belle' sets strayed; there were three recorded occasions when sets ran from Waterloo to Portsmouth on specials, one

The 1927 car *Rainbow II* was burnt out at Micheldever in 1936; 16 years later Preston Park turned out *Phoenix* using what was left, and providing a stylish modern car which was much used in Royal and VIP trains; here seen outside the depot in May 1952.

Avery Brighton

Neptune was a kitchen car of 1921 built at Longhedge; it was later third class No. 15 and finally a camping coach, and is probably here back at Longhedge for conversion at that time.

Lens of Sutton

a 'Royal' for the then Princess Elizabeth. Two Pullman trains appeared in London Docks in February 1954 when a strike diverted a liner from Southampton; the route from Waterloo was circuitous and no doubt the trains caused astonishment passing through Dudding Hill and Putney Bridge. Two other notable trains are worth a mention: a train of 12 first class Pullmans from Victoria to Erith for a works visit, and a Lourdes Pilgrim Train with Pullman kitchen cars interspersed with WD ambulance coaches.

Two other Pullman specials of 1953 were unusual; firstly they ran from Southampton to Victoria, and there was no easy route, there being no connection at Clapham Junction or via the West London Railway for the main line, and a rather sordid route via Wimbledon, Tooting and Streatham Junction was usually chosen. Secondly, they were carrying passengers from the cruise liner *Carortia* to view the Coronation, and this involved the trains leaving the Docks about 4 am! In the mid-1950s, a rather attenuated Royal Train was noted on several occasions, comprising two 'Restriction O' brake coaches each side of the Pullman *Aquila*; however the Royal race train to Tattenham Corner was always four-car.

The Region had now gone a long way towards fixed-interval trains on all services, and therefore the tally of Pullman services can be simply presented, for instance for the 1955/6 winter table:

Central Section: Brighton Line: trains with Pullmans ran on the hour from Victoria from 9 am to midnight, the 11 am and 3 and 7 pm workings being the all-Pullman 'Brighton Belle'. Exceptions were the 5 pm 'City Limited' which ran from London Bridge, as also a 6.05 pm which split at Haywards Heath, the Pullman-equipped portion going on to Brighton and that with a pantry car to Littlehampton. Littlehampton trains were at 25 minutes past, from 9.25 am to 7.25 pm; however, the 12.25 was SO and there was no 1.25 or 6.25. There was also a 10.45 pm shared with the Hastings line, splitting at Haywards Heath. Eastbourne and Hastings line; hourly at 45 minutes past from 8.45 am to 10.45 pm, but the 1.45 was SO; also a midnight train shared with Brighton. The 9.05 am boat train to Newhaven also included a Pullman.

Western Section: 12.30 Waterloo to Bournemouth (all-Pullman). Also Southampton boat trains.

Eastern Section: 11.35 am Victoria to Ramsgate was a supplement train, any composites working on other lines counted as refreshment cars only. The Dover continental train now ran at 10 am from Victoria, the Folkestone trains being at 12.30 and 1 pm, the latter being the 'Golden Arrow' at this time running via Folkestone instead of Dover. The former carried Ostend passengers, who also had a 9 am with Pullmans.

In 1959 a new coat of arms was adopted by the company. Put in non-heraldic language, the only difference seemed to be that the lions supporting the shield were horizontal rather than vertical. The company was now in the throes of a face-lift which had been agreed in 1955, namely the introduction of multiple-unit diesel Pullman trains, intended for businessmen's routes. The new trains, in six-car sets for the London Midland Region and eight-car for the Western, appeared in 1960, in a new blue livery, with a grey stripe, changed later to grey with a blue stripe. These trains were very rare visitors to the SR, but sets were noted at Salisbury on 25th April, 1970, at Brockenhurst on 25th March, 1971, and

Plato was a 1927 MCW kitchen car, used in the Royal Train to Epsom races in 1947.
Lens of Sutton

Grosvenor was a kitchen car on the 1908 'Southern Belle', but was withdrawn in 1936 and converted to a bar car, for the Newhaven boat trains.   *Lens of Sutton*

at Ashford on 21st July, 1972. In 1966 when the ex-LMS main line was electrified, the two 'Manchester Pullman' trains were redundant, and they were offered to all the other Regions. The Eastern seems to have said no after a trial, the Southern without a trial, and they went to the Western.

In 1958 the six former Hastings line cars plus the *Hadrian Bar* (former Car No. 59), were sold to British Rail (Southern Region) and painted green without names, lettered 'Buffet' and with the schedule numbers (180-185) on the sides. In 1961 these were numbered into SR stock, S7872S to S7877S in the following order: *Camilla, Latona, Theodora, Madeline, Pomona, Barbara* (schedule numbers 180, 181,184, 182,183,185). The Hadrian Bar was numbered S7879S. They were used mainly on the Southampton Boat Trains, the last of which with a Pullman ran in June 1963; the 'green Pullmans' were also all withdrawn by that time.

On 11th June, 1961 the 'Golden Arrow' was electric-hauled for the first time, the great conversion of the old SER main line being completed. This was also a time of many line closures, and some 'last trains' featured Pullmans. There was one on the last train over the Kent & East Sussex Railway on 11th June, 1961 (though a few years later the new Tenterden Railway would own two Pullmans and trains would run again). The first and last all-Pullman train on the Somerset & Dorset Railway ran in December 1961 to Blandford Forum. The company also sensed the need to preserve something, and took *Topaz* (I) out of service to restore it to original 1914 form (though not livery) complete with a pair of 1913 bogies; it went for a time to the Clapham Transport Museum in London.

In the autumn of 1963 an extra run each way was put on for the 'Brighton Belle'; the down run was at 11 pm and the stock was brought into Victoria at 10 pm for late dinners. However by this time the Pullman Company was really no more; in 1962 the BTC had purchased the remaining shares, and on 1st January, 1963 the BTC became British Railways Board, with Pullman being in effect a part of the British Transport Hotels & Catering. The 'Belle' continued to be in the news; on 18th August, 1963 faster running was tried, and a trip done in 51½ minutes; but the verdict was that it was too rough for the public. Then on 28th March, 1964 Charter Trains Ltd began to charter the 'Belle' at week-ends for 'a night of gambling at Brighton'. This did not last long; no doubt its presence in the small hours when the maintenance people felt they ought to have the line was an irritant - on occasion it was locomotive-hauled with ER Pullmans 'owing to electric power not being available', and also diverted via Shoreham.

The 1928 LNER car *Joan*, which had been put at Winston Churchill's disposal during the War, and was later much used by General Eisenhower, had come to the SR in 1960, and when the General was visiting Britain in 1962, this car was sent up to the Midland Region for a sentimental (and press-covered) reunion.

From May 1965 the 'Golden Arrow' became officially a mixed rather than all-Pullman train, a recognition in fact of a state of affairs which had occurred on occasion before this date. From 12th April, 1965 Pullmans were withdrawn from the 'mixed' 'Talisman' trains from Kings Cross to Newcastle, Edinburgh and Glasgow.

What was probably the most-publicised Pullman train ever ran on 30th January, 1965 - the funeral train for Winston Churchill, which was on the SR from Waterloo as far as Reading. The cars used were *Carina, Lydia, Perseus,* and *Isle of Thanet*, the coffin being in bogie van No. S2464 painted in Pullman livery.

Sometimes Pullman trains were noted in unusual places. This 'Bournemouth Belle' hauled by a Brush type '4' and without roofboards is climbing out of Alton having been diverted by engineering works. *J. Scrace*

This car seen in an unhappy state at Cardiff in 1972 was formerly *Rosalind* on the SECR. It was later a NAAFI canteen and camping coach; here it carries the service department number DW150431. Finally it has been preserved. *D. Gould*

Two former 'Brighton Belle' motor cars, in the grey livery, await their fate at Manningtree in March 1976; all six motor coaches later found homes. *D. Gould*

The same year saw the beginning of withdrawal of the 6-PUL sets from the former LBSC main lines, to be replaced by 4-COR units which had no Pullmans. The last 6-PUL ran on 24th April, 1966, and the Pullman presence on the Brighton line was now confined to the 'Belle'. On 9th July, 1967 the 'Bournemouth Belle' also went, and again the new electric stock did not include Pullmans.

There were still a few Pullmans in service on the Eastern Section boat trains: 306 *Orion*, 302 *Phoenix*, 301 *Perseus*, 305 *Aquila*, 307 *Carina*, 247 *Isle* of *Thanet*, and Car 208. As stated earlier, in 1964 the official Pullman livery had been changed to grey with a broad blue stripe covering the window area, but the Southern Region elected to paint most of their cars in BR livery, and the 'Brighton Belle' appeared first in this livery in November 1968. The name of the train appeared where the old car names had been, and the schedule number at each end of the lower portion; first class cars had a large figure '1' on the doors. A similar treatment was applied to 'Golden Arrow' cars. The Southern Region timetable still made passing reference to Pullmans, the London-Paris section having certain trains keyed as 'first class accommodation is provided only in Pullman cars and second class only in ordinary carriages'. However, the entries on the Brighton line table for the four 'Belle' trips made no mention of Pullmans.

There were still nine trains on BR which were all-Pullman or nearly so, but eight would be taken off in the next 10 years. The first to go was the 'Brighton Belle', on 30th April, 1972, no doubt because it was the oldest stock by far. The next was the 'Golden Arrow' on 30th September, 1972, because electric multiple units had proved more handy, and what passengers thought of the trains was no longer considered important. So although so-called Pullmans in various blue liveries would go on running for a few years on other parts of the railway system, for the Southern Region it was the end of the Pullman. However, they were certainly not going with a whimper. Tribute to the 'Brighton Belle' began even before public service ended: a 'Brighton Belle Commemoration Tour' was run on 1st April, 1972, in the course of which set 3053 ran from Waterloo to Victoria via Portsmouth, Eastbourne and Brighton.

The last day of the 'Brighton Belle', 30th April, 1972, was 'celebrated' in style. There had been enormous objection to the ending of this Pullman train, and it, must be said that the earlier decision to paint it in BR livery after 60 years in umber and cream, when it was known to have only a few years to go, showed gross insensitivity. Anyway, on the day, in addition to the three timetabled runs each way, there was an extra up run at 18.50 for a wine and cheese party (£7.50), and an extra down run at 22.30 for a 'Champagne Special' (£10). Finally on 9th May there was a 'musical excursion', also with champagne. There was also great concern at rumours that all three trains were to be sold to America, though in the event all cars were sold as separate items and bought by UK people. In October 1972 five 'Golden Arrow' Pullmans were offered for sale, Nos. 301/2, 306-8. They were moved from Stewarts Lane depot to Lovers Walk, Brighton, where they joined some unsold 'Brighton Belle' cars, though some of these had already left in an undignified way by freight train, as No. 288 did via Norwood and Temple Mills to Clacton. Cars 285-7 and 291-3 were bought as a block by Allied Breweries, but were destined to spend some 12 months in sidings first as Mistley and then at Manningtree.

Lorna was one of the cars run as composites in the '6PUL' electric sets serving Brighton, Eastbourne and Hastings from 1933; this car was in set 2008, and is here seen at Eastbourne in 1965.

A. Swain

Pegasus was built in 1951 as a bar car for the 'Golden Arrow', named 'Trianon Bar'. It was later used on the Night Sleeper from Euston and renamed 'Nightcap Bar'.

Lens of Sutton

Table Three - Pullman cars coming to SR lines after 1927 list

Adrian	1928 K O		Lady Dalziel	1930 Bk G
Alice	1932 B C K		Loraine	1928 K O
Anne	1932 B C K		Lorna	1932 C B K
Aquilla	1951 G G K		Lucille	1928 L P
Aries	1951 GG K			
Audrey	1932 B K		Maid of Kent (II)[2]	
			May	1932 B C K
Bertha	1932 B C K		Mona	1932 B K
Brenda	1932 B C K			
			Naomi	1932 B C K
Carina	1951 G G K			
Clara	1932 B C K		Olive	1932 B C K
Cygnus	1951 G G P		Onyx	1932 B C K
			Orion	1951 GG K
Daisy	1932 B C K			
Diamond	1928 G K		Pearl	1924 G K
Doris	1932 B K		Peggy	1932 B C K
			Pegasus	1951 Bar GG
Elinor	1932 B C K		Penelope	1928 L P
Enid	1932 B C K		Perseus	1951 GG P
Ethel	1932 B C K		Phyllis	1928 L P
Eunice	1928 G O P		Philomel	1928 L P
Evadne	1928 K O		Phoenix	1951 GG P[3]
			Princess Elizabeth	1930 B L O P
Grace	1932 B C K			
Gwladys	1932 B C K		Rainbow (II)[4]	
Gwen	1932 B K		Rita	1932 B C K
			Rose	1932 B C K
Hazel	1932 B K		Ruth	1932 B C K
Hercules	1951 GG P			
			Ursula	1928 L P
Ida	1932 B C K			
Ione	1928 G K O		Vera	1932 B K
Iris	1932 B C K		Violet	1932 B C K
Isle of Thanet[1]				
			Zena	1928 O P
Joan	1928 O P			
Joyce	1932 B C K			
Juana	1928 O P			

'Brighton Belle' sets were:

3051: 88	Hazel	Doris	86	89
3052: 90	Vera	Audrey	87	91
3053: 92	Gwen	Mona	85	93

Third/Second Class Cars

No. 40	(1921) Bk LE P W	No. 96	see *Sylvia*
No. 41	(1920) Bk LE P W	No. 97	see *Calais*
No. 45	(1920) K L 12	No. 98	see *Milan*
No. 47	(1920) K L 12	No. 99	see *Padua*
No. 54	(1923) Bk LE P	No. 132	see *Anaconda*
No. 55	(1923) Bk LE P	No. 133	see *Erminie*
No. 60	(1928) K W	No. 135	see *Elmira*
No. 61	(1928) K LE	No. 137	see *Maid of Kent* II
No. 63	(1928) Bk LE P	No. 153	see *Aurora*
No. 65	(1925) K LE	No. 154	see *Flora*
No. 75	(1928) L P	No. 161	see *Fortuna* (K ex-ER)
No. 76	(1928) L P	No. 162	see *Irene* (K ex-ER)
No. 81	(1931) Bk P W	No. 166	see *Geraldine*
No. 82	(1931) Bk L P W	No. 167	see *Marjorie*
No. 83	(1931) P W	No. 169	see *Viking*
No. 84	(1931) L P W	No. 171	see *Pauline*
No. 85-7	(1932) B P	No. 181-5	ex-Hastings cars, see text
No. 88-93	(1982) B Bk M P	No. 194	see Car 36
No. 94	(1920) Bk P 12	No. 208	see *Leona*
	ex-ER *Ansonia*	No. 248	see *Lady Dalziel*
No. 95	(1920) Bk P 12 ex-ER	No. 249	see *Pearl*
	Arcadia	No. 303	new 1952, K GG

Notes

B - 1932 Brighton electric, Bk - brake or guard, C - composite, G - 1928 'Golden Arrow', GG - 1951 'Golden Arrow', K - kitchen or buffet, L - ex-LNER 1928 all-steel, LE - earlier ex-LNER, M - motored, O - ex-GWR cars, 1930, P - parlour, W - 1931 'Bournemouth Belle'.

1 *Isle of Thanet* renaming of *Princess Elizabeth*.
2 *Maid of Kent* II renaming of *Formosa*.
3 *Phoenix* reconstruction of *Rainbow* I.
4 *Rainbow* II renaming of *Cosmo Bonsor*.

It is believed that cars 34-6 ran for a time as 192-4 (2nd class).
Some other cars appear in records as second class but no photograph of a car lettered 'Second Class' is known.
Emerald was renumbered Second Class Car No. 1 about 1944, later instruction car 101.
Juno and *Aurora* briefly carried second class Nos. 502/3 in 1950.

Third class No. 63 was built by Midland C&W in 1928 as a dining car for LNER services, and rebuilt at Preston Park in 1950 as a brake parlour. It is seen here at Clapham Junction in August 1964 in the final livery and lining out for brake cars before the change to blue/grey was adopted.   *J.H. Meredith*

Chapter Eight

British Rail's 1960/1966 Cars and Diesels

By the mid-1950s it was felt that given new rolling stock, the number of all-Pullman trains could be increased on the fast East Coast route of the Eastern Region, and tenders were put out for 44 new cars. Metro-Cammell was successful in attracting the order, for seven first class parlours, 13 first class kitchens, eight second class parlours and 15 second class kitchens, plus a second class bar.

The design was based on the BR Mark I underframe and shell, but had 'Commonwealth' bogies with roller bearings; the windows were enlarged and double-glazed. The new cars first appeared on the 'Master Cutler' in September 1960, in simplified Pullman livery and a redesigned crest.

Nos. 311-323 were first class kitchen cars, 324-31 first class parlours, 332-46 second class kitchen cars, 347-53 third class parlours. No. 354 was the 'Hadrian Bar' for the 'Tees-Tyne Pullman'; a replacement for the old Car 59 of the same name, it later became the 'Night Cap Bar' on the 'Night Limited' to Glasgow.

The first class cars were given names, some of which had been used before:

311	*Eagle*	315	*Heron*	319	*Snipe*	323	*Wren*	327	*Garnet*
312	*Falcon*	316	*Magpie*	320	*Stork*	324	*Amber*	328	*Opal*
313	*Finch*	317	*Raven*	321	*Swift*	325	*Amethyst*	329	*Pearl*
314	*Hawk*	318	*Robin*	322	*Thrush*	326	*Emerald*	330	*Ruby*
								331	*Topaz*

In the 1960s Pullmans were still very popular with railway managements, especially perhaps the North Eastern Region, which in its book of tables gave four pages to its trains, the 'White Rose' serving Wakefield, Leeds, Bradford and Harrogate; the 'Tees-Tyne' for York, Darlington and Newcastle; the 'Harrogate Sunday Pullman'; and the 'Yorkshire Pullman', from Harrogate, whose Hull portion was allowed to pick up at Brough, but not to set down on the up journey, and vice versa on the down one. The 'Master Cutler' for Sheffield was for some reason only publicised in the Eastern Region timetable book. This train, which ran with ordinary stock from Marylebone from 1947, and was re-routed to Kings Cross as all-Pullman in 1948, was formed of ordinary stock again from 7th October, 1968. It had also been diverted from Sheffield Victoria to Midland in October 1965.

The 'Tees-Tyne' was not one of the best-known Pullman trains, but in the 1960s it began to assume importance as Tees-side industry built up. Timings were frequently changed, and there was annoyance when the down train was timed to miss the Saltburn connection at Darlington by one minute. Regulars expected accelerations when diesels came in, but in fact they could not better the performance of an 'A4' Pacific well-driven, until the 'Deltics' arrived in 1964. In that year Tees-side Airport was opened which provided competition, but the down train was often full, and first class cars had their seating altered and second class cars were taken off. Also taken off was the 'Hadrian Bar', inherited from the 'Queen of Scots', a successor to Car 59 which had carried the same name.

Above: This close-up of 1960 car No. 334 shows the altered Pullman coat of arms and the new type bogies adopted on this series. *Lens of Sutton*

Right: This diagram of Pullman train services was included in the BR timetables in all regions in 1966.

From January 1961 the train was formed from 1960 Pullmans, necessarily in view of the speeds attained; in 1972 the late Derek Barrie obtained 100 mph while timing the down train, between Hitchin and Holme and also Grantham and Templehirst; speed did not drop below 86 mph up Stoke bank: 'Deltic' No. 9005 was hauling 11 Pullmans.

No provision had been made in the 1960 cars for luggage, and most trains used older 'end-cars'. For a time it seemed that the glory days of Pullmans had returned. But things were not really the same; the acquisition of the company by the BTC in 1962, and a later decision to abandon the old livery were bad omens. There was some indecision on the matter of the new livery; some cars ran in the standard BR livery of the time, while others adopted a different livery, grey with blue topside; the 'Yorkshire Pullman' was noted with two grey cars in February 1968.

The 'Queen of Scots' ran for the last time on 12th January, 1963; it had recently been formed from 1960 cars but with old end-cars, and hauled by a 'Deltic' diesel. On the 14th January the cars were transferred to the 'White Rose', a Harrogate train formerly using ordinary stock. Thus between London and Leeds the 'Queen's' Pullman facility was replaced. From September 1963 the 'Sunday Harrogate Pullman' also used new stock; this pre-War train remained running until 5th May, 1978.

Passengers for Scotland were now catered for by the blue 'Talisman' which ran twice per day in each direction. Some Pullmans were used on the working out of Kings Cross at 8 am until 22nd April, 1965, but this was not regarded as a Pullman train. British Rail (ER) had formed a policy of phasing out old Pullmans, and many were going for scrap, some at Forncett. Others were to have much further life; for example *Ione*, which had finished its service life on the 'Master Cutler', after spending some time at Peterborough East, was sold for £850 in October 1969, went to Birmingham Museum, and later joined the VSOE private train.

In 1972 the Eastern Region went in for the 'theming' of Pullman trains, with logos on the coach sides, stewards' badges and so on. However headboards, which had become less common after the Atlantic locomotives ceased to run, were not used. In spite of this, the trains were allowed to decline. The 'Yorkshire Pullman' on its last run on 5th May, 1978 had only four grey painted Pullmans with seven coaches in BR livery. The 'Tyne-Tees' ceased to run from 4th May, 1976; the 'Hull Pullman', withdrawn with the 'Yorkshire', ended up with only two cars in its formation.

A dozen withdrawn cars were noted in July 1974 stored at Rugby in a dilapidated state. Some were now on the former Great Eastern, used as open firsts and as diners on the Boat Trains; however Nos. E320 and E333 were on the 'Hull Pullman' in the summer of 1974, and No. E325 was on the Settle-Carlisle Centenary train on 1st May, 1976. The last seven cars were not withdrawn until January 1981.

By August 1975 12 cars had been moved from Derby to Kingmoor Yard, Carlisle, two in grey livery and the rest in old livery, with windows boarded against vandals. Some cars were now being used for departmental purposes; No. 335 was on the West Highland line for maintenance projects.

THE MIDLAND PULLMAN

A publicity photograph of the Midland Pullman in original Nanking blue livery; each end car had a 1,000 hp MAN engine.

A Blue Pullman is seen at Birmingham (Snow Hill) on 28th March, 1961. It has just arrived from Paddington with the 12.10 from Paddington and will later form the 2.30 pm return working. In the distance ex-GWR 2-8-0 No. 3831 can be seen 'light engine'. *Michael Mensing*

In 1981 eight remaining cars were moved to Carlisle Upperby depot and hired out for a special trains by the Steam Locomotive Owners' Association (*see Chapter Nine*). Many others were sold to private railways or for use as public houses etc. (*see Chapter Ten*).

The 'Blue Pullmans'

The reputation of the orthodox Pullmans was still riding high in 1960 when British Rail introduced its first diesel multiple unit sets bearing that title and with the Pullman coat of arms on the front. These trains were built by Metropolitan Vickers at Saltley, with two 1,000 hp NBL/MAN engines and GEC main generators, and were capable of 90 mph. The trailer cars were 65½ ft long (motors one foot longer) and 9 ft wide. Two six-car trains were ordered, for the St Pancras-Manchester ex-Midland line, it being intended to use the trains in the middle of the day for a return run from London to Leicester. These were all-first and seated 132. Three eight-car sets had extra 'Parlour cars' for second class next to the motor coaches and seated 108 first class and 120 second. These were to be used on the Western Region between Paddington and Wolverhampton and Bristol. The third eight-car set was supposed to be a 'spare', but was later used on a 'South Wales Pullman' train to Swansea, leading to two trains of orthodox Pullmans being formed to cover maintenance withdrawals of sets.

The livery was Nanking blue with a broad white band along the windows; there was air-conditioning and heat insulation. As usual with Pullmans, the internal decor varied. Riding comfort was to be ensured by the use of Metro-Schlieren bogies having helical springs. The two motor bogies at each end of the sets were placed one under the inner end of the motor coach, and the other under the adjacent end of the next coach, kitchen cars in the six-car sets, and parlour cars in the eight-car version.

The first public 'Midland Pullman' ran on 14th July, 1960. The Nottingham service was planned to start on 1st January, 1961, but the Union refused to work the mid-day train beyond Leicester and the extended Nottingham service did not begin until 2nd October.

The Western Region's 'Birmingham Pullman' first ran on 12th September, 1960, and the 'Bristol Pullman' on the same day. Initially the morning 'Midland' train ran from Wolverhampton to Paddington in 2 hrs 35 min.; the midday train missed out Solihull and turned round at Snow Hill. The morning up Bristol train reached Paddington in 1 hr 50 min and ran via Badmington. The second working ran via Bath and called there. The 'South Wales Pullman', a diesel version of an orthodox Pullman train begun on 27th June, 1955, had its first run on 11th September, 1961, between Paddington and Swansea. Because there was now no set not in daily use, in 1964/5 the sets were in turn taken in for heavy overhaul, a 'scratch' set of orthodox Pullmans was made up, and a second one later. Passengers soon complained that most of these were old second class cars, and it was necessary to have nine second class cars repainted as 'first' and give them names. These cars were as follows:

Car	Pullman Register	Name
66	188	*Avon*
73	226	*Ceteia*
105	210	*Hebe*
74	227	*Melandra*
60	215	*Severn*
106	211	*Thalia*
61	216	*Thames*
109	212	*Thetis*
35	193	*Wye*

The earlier relief train had comprised four second class Pullmans, first class *Cecilia* and two non-Pullman coaches; it ran between 26th February and 12th March, 1962. Cars 105/106/109 had previously been named *Marcelle/ Sybil/Kathleen* before earlier demotions.

The first train to be treated, the 'Bristol Pullman', which was withdrawn for overhaul on 8th May, 1964 had run 370,000 miles. On its return the train had an intermediate (middle-day) working to Weston-super-Mare. The 'Birmingham Pullman' was withdrawn as soon as the Bristol one was back in service.

When in 1966 the Manchester line was electrified and locomotive-hauled Pullmans provided, some 'blue' sets become spare, and the 'Bristol Pullman' was made a 12-car train except for the mid-day working. As they did not run at the week-ends, they were much used for excursions and private trains, being noted for instance at Aintree, West Hartlepool and Norwich. An 'Oxford Pullman' was put on from 6th March, 1967, which ran until 2nd May, 1969. The 'Birmingham Pullman' ceased to run from 3rd March, 1967.

Hire cost for an 8-coach train in 1966 was £1,200. In 1972 a train was hired for a tour from Guildford via Reading, Carmarthen, Salisbury, Basingstoke and Woking.

In 1968 the Nanking blue livery had been abandoned and grey livery with blue window surrounds substituted. The last public working of the 'South Wales Pullman' was on 4th May, 1973; however a commemorative train was run the following day, outwards by an unusual route via Leamington and over the former LNWR to Coventry, then New Street, Cheltenham, Bristol and so to Swansea.

The sets were stored at Old Oak and Bristol St Phillips Marsh, though one motor coach was stationed at Temple Meads as a relief generator. For scrapping the 36 cars were split between Cohen's yard at Swansea and Thomas Ward at Briton Ferry. No immediate action was taken, and in April 1975 a consortium planned to purchase power cars Nos. 60090/1, kitchen firsts 60731/3 and second saloons 60644/5-9 from the breakers. However, British Rail would not allow them, if operated, to leave the Western Region, and it was considered not viable for that reason. The reason given by BR was that other Regions had no drivers trained to operate them, though this perhaps could have been overcome.

Midland Region Locomotive-Hauled Pullmans

Going back to the 1960s, it was decided to bring back Pullmans to the former LMS, and in 1966 29 new cars, all first class, were delivered for a new 'Manchester Pullman' and 'Liverpool Pullman'. These were virtually BR Mk II carriages with some extras, and were numbered 500-5 (kitchen), 540-53 (parlour) and 581-6 (brakes). The new trains began running from 18th April, 1966; however the Liverpool train was not very successful and was deleted from the timetables on 5th May, 1975.

Both trains ran twice daily; initially the first Manchester train left Euston at 07.50 and the Liverpool one at 07.45. The morning run from Manchester was at 07.50 and that from Liverpool Lime Street 07.55. The down Manchester served to pick up at Watford and to set down at Stockport Edgeley; the second train of the day performed the same service for Wilmslow, and the Liverpool train served Watford and Runcorn in the same way. All these trains were weekdays-only. The Liverpool one included some ordinary 'third' stock.

In 1983, though almost life-expired the cars were refurbished and relaunched with great hype, the new 'Manchester Pullman' running from 5th October, 1983, and a new 'Liverpool Pullman' from May 1984. The former train was all first, but the latter had only four first class cars in each set, the remainder being ordinary seconds. In both cases two rakes were in use. Each car carried the name of some past or present northern notable on a red band below the window, the main livery being grey with dark blue window surrounds. Most received different names in a further re-launch in 1985, and renamed again in the private sector (*see Chapter Nine and Appendix Three*).

The former 'Hadrian Bar' (car 354) now renumbered M354E was retitled 'Nightcap Bar' and ran in the 'Night Limited' sleeper service from London to Glasgow until October 1980; it was later noted on the 'Cumbrian Mountain Express'.

The 'Manchester Pullman' stock was withdrawn from that service in 1985, the last trip being on 10th May. It was replaced by Inter-City Mk IIIB stock. The former cars were to be available for charter work, and in autumn 1986 it was decided that a series of charters would be run to the Lake District; accordingly the cars were suitably renamed and the first Special was launched by the South Lakeland Council in a ceremony at Oxenholme on 20th May, 1987.

The new names were: 504 *Ullswater*, 506 *Windermere*, 546 *Coniston Water*, 548 *Grasmere*, 549 *Bassenthwaite*, 550 *Rydal Water*, 551 *Buttermere*, 552 *Ennerdale Water*, 553 *Crummock Water*, 586 *Derwent Water*.

A number of new 'Pullman' trains were announced in 1985, with names such as 'Merseysider', 'Lancashire', 'Scottish', and new 'Yorkshire' and 'Master Cutler' Pullmans, all HST stock. The word now simply meant 'super first class' and marked the end of the provision of the railways' long association with vehicles aiming to stand out from the crowd. The continuing use of Pullmans as enthusiasts had known them lay with private trains.

Derby had been asked for 38 Mk IIIB open firsts, and 22 (Nos. 11073-11094) were designated 'Pullmans'. These were allocated names of important North Country people as before, but only 10 of the 1983 names were re-used, some important ones being 'ditched'; this is the more surprising since cars 11075/80/90 did not carry any name. The whole idea of naming seems to have become unpopular, and from 1991 they were removed, making the 'Pullmans' appear the same as other open firsts. The word Pullman continued to be used to signify superior service, but was no longer attached only to a certain type of carriage.

On 13th May, 1985 the 'Manchester Pullman', which the previous Friday had comprised 1966 Pullmans, was switched to Mk III 'pretend' Pullmans. It was encouraging that the name was still around, but it was a confusing picture. When in November a ceremony took place at Euston to unveil the name of *Sir Stanley Matthews* above the Pullman coat of arms on the side of coach No. 11091, the real Pullmans of the VSOE were running regularly, and the 1960 cars (not real Pullmans in some eyes) were also busy outside BR control, with trains such as the 'Welsh Marches Belle' (Hereford to Gloucester) and the 'Cumbrian Mountain Express'. The 1966 cars ran on charter trains for BR, but the last of these, the 'Copy Pit Pullman' ran on 29th December, 1990, after which the cars were put up for sale.

As in 1983, with the launch of a Pullman Club and tie, in 1986 BR announced 'a revival of the Pullman tradition' in a lavish brochure, promising 'Pullman chefs on board' and a Pullman Club at Euston. A map indicated Pullman trains from Kings Cross to Newcastle and Bradford, and from Euston to Manchester, Liverpool and Blackpool. Other stations with regular Pullman services were given as Watford, Stafford, Stoke, Doncaster, Leeds, York, Darlington, Durham, Runcorn, Stockport, Wilmslow, Macclesfield, New Pudsey and Wakefield Westgate.

And so in its last few years before meltdown, British Rail kept up this front, though not all passengers were impressed. Since privatisation, the idea of super-luxury is still around, in a welter of new liveries, not all in good taste. The author is grateful that one livery which he has been familiar with for 70 years is still with us, on the VSOE. Long may it continue.

The remaining former 1966 Pullmans were officially transferred to private owners' stock in January 1992 and renumbered as below:

546	99670	*City Of Manchester*	551	99674	*Caledonian*
548	99671	*Elizabethan*	552	99675	*Southern Belle*
549	99672	*Prince Rupert*	553	99676	*King Arthur*
550	99673	*Royal Highlander*	586	99677	*Talisman*

These names took the place of the Lakeland ones, and were adopted in September 1991.

Chapter Nine

Private Pullman Trains

In 1968 Bulmers Cider purchased five Pullmans for £3,600 and stationed them at its Hereford depot together with GWR 4-6-0 No. 6000 *King George V*. A promotional tour of England was made in Spring 1969, but BR refused to allow No. 6000 to run as 'it would be psychologically upsetting for the public to see a steam engine'. However later it was allowed to run, and there was a special effort in October 1971; initially there was a round of four runs, taking in Newport, Oxford, Leamington, Banbury, Birmingham, Bicester and Swindon. They ran in Bulmers own livery, green white and red. They were given names as follows:

Hermione	became	*Morella*
Car 83	became	*Prinie*
Car 64	became	*Christine*
Car 76	became	*Eve*
Aquila	kept her name	

These cars were seen all over the system on hire for enthusiasts trips; however in the mid-1980s BR requirements regarding private stock on their lines became more stringent, and the cars were disposed of, *Morella* and *Aquila* to the Colne Valley Railway, *Prinie* and *Christine* to the Bluebell Railway, and *Eve* to the VSOE. This left only *Ruth*, a later acquisition from the former SR electric stock, at the Hereford depot.

The best-known private Pullman train was the Venice-Simplon-Orient Express (VSOE) run by Sea Containers Ltd, which ran two or three trips per week from Victoria to Dover, and was used for various excursions at other times. The first regular Continental trip was on 28th May, 1982. The stock comprised fairly old Pullmans either purchased direct or from static exhibition. The original cars were *Cygnus, Carina, Perseus, Audrey, Ibis, Phoenix, Minerva* and *Zena*. *Phoenix* and *Carina* had been across the channel earlier and spent some years as restaurants at Lyons. As time went on, the VSOE had problems with its wooden-bodied cars and arranged 'swops' with other owners who had steel-bodied cars but did not use them hard in service: former 'Belle' car *Vera*, which had served as a summer-house in Suffolk from 1972, was purchased by VSOE in 1985 and after very careful restoration went into service in 1991. In 1992 'Belle' motor unit 288 which had been at Swanage, was bought by VSOE for possible future use in a 'push-pull' Pullman train. Cars 92/3 (ex-'Brighton Belle') were added in 1996.

The oldest preserved car was *Cambria*, a former Great Eastern Continental buffet car, a 12-wheeler. It arrived at the Kent & East Sussex Railway in 1980 in poor shape after having been a mess and tool van at Sheffield. The Kent & East Sussex Railway was the first private line to run Pullman specials, using former Hastings cars *Theodora* and *Barbara*; a third 'Pullman' named *Diana* was made up from a

The Bulmers Cider Pullman train stationed at their Hereford depot along with *King George V* made many trips over the main lines; here at Radley in October 1971. The leading car was formerly third class Car 83. *R.J. Farrell*

A VSOE train arrives at Tunbridge Wells West behind class '33' No. 33 042 on 2nd October, 1984. *P.G. Barnes*

restaurant car. The K&ESR also mounted an exhibition at Tenterden to honour the sesquicentenary of the birth of George Mortimer Pullman on 31st March, 1831. During this, on 8th August, Julian Morel, former Pullman Co. Catering Manager, named the new 'fake' Pullman *Diana*; the exhibition had been opened by Col F. Harding, Pullman Co. Managing Director. A 1960 car was leased in 1995.

The Strathspey Railway at Aviemore ran a short dining train, with Pullman *Amethyst* attached to the buffet car named *Glenfiddich*.

The most publicly visible private Pullman trains were those of the Steam Locomotive Operators' Association, set up in 1975, which purchased eight 1960 Pullmans from BR in 1981, which had become surplus on the East Coast trains. In addition the 'Night Cap Bar' (former 'Hadrian Bar') was taken over. The train was dual-heated, and was maintained under contract by BR at Carlisle (Upperby) depot.

The Steam Locomotive Operators' Association took over their 1960 cars to provide opportunities for steam runs on main lines, which had been agreed with British Rail, but the reactions of enthusiasts to the first runs were not all good. They complained that the cars were hard to see out of, and they could not put their heads out of the windows to hear the engine working. 'Bring back the Mark I stock' many said. The SLOA pointed out that they had provided half-brakes at one end for people who wanted to make tape recordings of steam sounds, and that if they did not provide modern stock, BR would not allow the trains on the main lines. In 1983 the Midland Region's summer scheme was taken over by the SLOA; 14 specials were planned, including the 'Cumbrian Mountain Pullman', 'Cumbrian Coast Pullman' and 'Welsh Marches Pullman'. Normally they left Euston at 8 am and returned at 10 pm. With breakfast, lunch and dinner the cost was around £40; however the VSOE train was even more expensive: £90 for a Saturday run to the Beaulieu Motor Museum.

Repainting in traditional livery was carried out at Steamtown, Carnforth; later however the cars had to go to BR Bounds Green to have asbestos stripped out. In the early 1990s the use of private coaches on the main lines was restricted to those carrying a plate on the solebar confirming they could be hauled at 100 mph; the 1960 cars could not meet this and were stored for a time at Ferme Park sidings.

The 1960 cars were also used on several private railways. Six were purchased by Michael Bayliss in 1983 and sent via Taunton to the Severn Valley Railway for a 'wine and dine' train. The West Somerset Railway at Minehead had used these cars in 1981/2. Three cars were loaned to the Swanage Railway and renamed: 335 *Linnette*, 348 *Iseult*, 353 *Melisande*. Cars 318, 327 and 328 were on the North Yorkshire Moors Railway in 1981; No. 325 had been on the Strathspey Railway since 1978.

In 1989 the Great Scottish & Western Railway purchased the six cars previously used on the West Somerset Railway (*Amber, Finch, Raven, Pearl, Snipe, Topaz*) and after asbestos had been stripped at Hull Dairycoates these were placed on the 'Royal Scotsman' Fort William-Mallaig train. *Amber* was renamed 'State Car No. 1'; *Pearl* was No. 2, *Topaz* 3 and *Finch* 4; *Snipe* became an observation car. No doubt these 1960 cars will continue to move around; it is of interest that those preserved are running on five different types of bogie, as BR in most cases did not allow modern bogies to be sold with the car, substituting

Class '73' electro-diesel No. 73 101 is seen painted in Pullman livery and carrying a headboard reading 'Brighton Belle' with a rake of VSOE Pullmans approaching Lovers Walk road bridge on 21st September, 1991.   *P.G. Barnes*

'Merchant Navy' class Pacific No. 35028 *Clan Line* approaches Gillingham Depot level crossing with the 9.30 am Victoria-Dover VSOE train on 9th June, 1996.   *P.G. Barnes*

ones which were older but still fit to be 'plated'. The plating system was devised to keep unfit cars off the main lines. Each preserved car of suitable type was allotted a number, placed on the sole bar.

Many 'preserved' cars have led a more exciting life than they did in regular service. Some swopping, buying and lending took place, resulting in cars moving long distances by rail or road. *Agatha* and *Fingall*, after their short stay at the Beaulieu Museum, crossed to the Isle of Wight, but seven years later returned back across the water to serve the Orient Express and the Bluebell Railway respectively. *Topaz* (I), restored by the Pullman Co. in 1961 for preservation, had most of the inside torn out again in 1979 to serve as an exhibition saloon in the touring train commemorating the centenary of the dining car, and in 1986 was 'restored' again, this time in the original 1913 lake livery. Some were genuinely static and may remain so, though a few clocked up short mileages: *Doris* took time off from duty as a businessman's dining room at Finsbury Park station to visit Derby in 1975 for repainting in original livery. *Orion* went to Wolverton for a similar purpose in 1978; *Aurora* and *Alicante* did the short trip from Fowey to Marazion in 1964 when WR camping coaches were concentrated at that place.

The two 'Devon Belle' observation cars had perhaps the most varied lives of all. It will be recalled that they had originally been ambulance cars on the LNWR in 1918, converted to Pullmans in 1921, and rebuilt as bar cars in 1937. In 1946 they were remodelled as observation cars, and were sold in 1957 to BR. No. 14 was put on the Glasgow-Oban run as Sc281. No. 13 became M280 and was on the North Wales Land Cruise, later (1961) going to Scotland as Sc280 on the Kyle of Lochalsh line, being joined there in 1967 by No. 14. No. 14 was sold again in 1969 and went overseas with the 'USA Flying Scotsman', ending up as a club in California. No. 13 was sold to the Torbay Railway for service on the Paignton line restored to Pullman livery; it has also worked on the associated Dart Valley line (now the South Devon Railway). Both cars seem to have carried BR livery in Scotland, though one was noted on excursions in the mid-1960s in a livery similar to Pullman but with BR logos and a long white stripe along the side, which it had also carried when owned by Pullman, with the words 'Pullman Observation Car' painted on it. No. 13 is now the oldest Pullman car in regular service, since the three older cars which have been preserved are static.

Ten VSOE Pullmans were plated as Nos. 99530-99541/3 (including three baggage cars). The Manchester Pullmans, known as the Carnforth Maroon Set, carried 99978-80, the last number being in fact the attendants' car, formerly 14102. The 'Royal Scotsman' train, run by Flying Scotsman Enterprises, contained former 1960 cars 324/9/31/13/19, 17, upgraded at Acton Works in 1994.

The former Manchester Pullmans (1966 vehicles) were for a time owned by Trainstour Ltd, but in 1991 were taken over by Manchester Executive Railway, afterwards called 'Statesman', and two cars were renamed yet again: 504 *White Rose*, 506 *Red Rose*.

The number of notable private Pullman workings is too many to give here; perhaps the many 'Cumbrian Mountain Pullman' trains are best remembered.

Left: First class electric kitchen car *Doris* became a Director's dining room at Finsbury Park. It is seen here in March 1977 after a repaint at Derby Works.   *D. Gould*

Below: After the last runs of the 'Devon Belle' in 1954 the two observation cars 13 and 14 were available for charter, and here one of them, probably 13, is tailing a 'Pennine Pullman' excursion at Sowerby Bridge in May 1956. Next year both were sold to BR.   *T. Lewis*

However there was also a spectacular 'Brighton Belle' in September 1991, for which class 73/1 locomotive No. 73 101 was painted in Pullman livery to haul the VSOE train; another special occasion in the same year saw seven Pullmans from the former Manchester rake working banked steam trains up and down the steep branch from Folkestone Harbour to Folkestone Junction all day.

By 1994 the former Manchester Pullman cars were in a new livery and without names, being run by the Great Scottish & Western Railway. It had been planned to run them as a luxury train to Blackpool under the aegis of Statesman Rail Ltd, but BR clearance could not be obtained.

In 1995 Pete Waterman, by now owner of nine 1960 Pullmans, offered them on free loan to private railways; Swanage took Nos. 335 and 353, and another went to a site at Okehampton. Two cars leased to BR for the one locomotive-hauled train in the Welsh Valleys are thought to have been from this batch, which under Waterman were running in black livery. A mini-bar car run by the Scottish Railway Preservation Society in 1983 as 'Car 1866' was in Pullman livery but was not in fact a former Pullman. Car 349 was leased to the Kent & East Sussex Railway to run on their Pullman dining train while their own *Barbara* was being overhauled, the first use being on a 'Santa Special' on 26th November, 1995. Shortly after, it was announced that the nine remaining 1960 cars had been purchased from Waterman by Dr Tony Marchington, with the hope of later restoring a complete 'Flying Scotsman' train on the main line.

There were further developments in 1996. The Statesman Railway Company, which had been operating the former Manchester Pullmans, ceased trading in November, and the cars passed to Regency Rail Cruises, associated with Steamtown, the first tour to be announced being one from Preston to Inverness in March 1997. At the end of the year Flying Scotsman Enterprises announced the addition of generator car 6312, made redundant from sleeping car trains, to its Pullman train, painted in Pullman livery.

Former Pullman cars remain in the news. The VSOE is always active; a three-day visit to Yorkshire in December 1997 brought it to places such as Scarborough and Appleby. Early in 1998 two former 'Brighton Belle' motor units, stored at Preston Park, and which the VSOE had purchased two years earlier, were moved to Stewarts Lane in badly vanadalised condition.

The 1928 car *Phyllis* which had been concealed for over a decade on a farm at Sellinge in Kent finally had her cover 'blown' and after sale was moved to the Bluebell Railway.

The cars parked at Marazion were also in the news when it was found that valuable panelling had been stolen from them.

A list of the present location of preserved Pullmans still on their bogies follows in Chapter Ten.

Chapter Ten

Preserved Pullmans

No railway rolling stock has ever seen such a high proportion of its number preserved, and most of the cars have seen further use in their proper role, and not as museum pieces, as shown in the previous chapter. In this chapter a list is given of all cars thought to be still on their bogies. There are also a number which were grounded and used in various ways; the identity and condition of most of these is known to the Pullman Society, but is not given here partly to preserve the privacy of the owners, and also because their present condition gives little clue as to their original appearance. It must also be emphasised that those still running are in many cases not on their original bogies and have had interior alterations.

Pre-1923 Cars

Alicante	Holiday coach at Fowey, later Marazion
Cambria	to K&ESR
Calais	Holiday coach, Marazion
Elmira	at Ravenglass R&ER
Formosa	at GCR Appletree Estate, Banbury
Maid of Kent (I)	Ravenglass R&ER
Malaga	at Ian Allan siding Shepperton
Mimosa	Holiday coach, Marazion
Padua	Pullman Lodge Hotel, Seaburn
Rosalind	Pullman Lodge Hotel, Seaburn
Sapphire	Pullman Lodge Hotel, Seaburn (formerly Ashford Steam Centre)
Topaz	National Railway Museum, York

(Observation Cars)

Car No. 13	Paignton & Dartmouth Railway
Car No. 14	San Francisco

Steam-hauled Cars 1923-51

Agatha	On VSOE (previously Beaulieu, IOW and Carnforth)
Aquila	Bulmers, from 1988 Colne Valley Railway
Aries	Yew tree Inn, Rochdale
Aurora	Holiday coach, Marazion (previously Fowey)
Barbara	on K&ESR
Carina	on VSOE
Cygnus	on VSOE
Fingall	on Bluebell Railway (formerly Beaulieu and Wight Railway)
Flora	Holiday coach, Marazion
Ibis	on VSOE (previously Tyseley)
Ione	on VSOE (previously Tyseley)
Juno	Holiday coach, Marazion
Leona	Cressing, Essex, later Elsenham
Lucille	on VSOE
Lydia	Wisconsin, USA
Minerva	on VSOE (previously Lytham Museum)
Montana	private use Cambridge
Orion	Peco, Beer, Devon
Perseus	on VSOE
Phoenix	on VSOE

Phyllis	from private to Bluebell Railway July 1997
Princess Elizabeth	Wisconsin
Theodora	on K&ESR
Ursula	Pub, Hilderstone, Staffs
Zena	on VSOE (previously Birmingham Transport Museum)
Car No. 36	*Hermione* on Colne Valley Railway; previously Bulmers
Car No. 54	on Bluebell Railway
Car No. 64	on Bluebell Railway
Car No. 75	Pub, Hilderstone, Staffs
Car No. 76	on VSOE (formerly Bulmers *Eve* to Bluebell Railway 1996)
Car No. 79	on North Yorkshire Moors Railway
Car No. 83	on VSOE (previously Bulmers)
Car No. 84	now *Mary* on Keighley & Worth Valley Railway

1933 Electric Cars

Audrey	private, then to VSOE
Bertha	Mid-Hants Railway then Bluebell
Doris	private, Finchley
Gwen	public house, Chingford, then Colne Valley Railway, then VSOE
Hazel	public house, Richmond, Yorks
Mona	public house, Winsford, Cheshire
Ruth	formerly Bulmers, Hereford
Vera	on VSOE (private 1972-85)
Car No. 85	public house, Mickleover, Derbys
Car No. 86	on VSOE
Car No. 87	North Norfolk Railway
Car No. 88	Stour Valley Railway, then Swanage, then VSOE
Car No. 89	public house, Rowarth, Derbys
Car No. 90	at Carnforth steam depot, formerly Nene Valley Railway
Car No. 91	North Norfolk Railway
Car No. 92	Preston Park depot; to Stewarts Lane 1998
Car No. 93	Preston Park depot; to Stewarts Lane 1998

1960 Cars

Amber	Great Scottish & Western Rly
Amethyst	Strathspey Rly
Eagle	National Railway Museum
Emerald (2)	National Railway Museum
Finch	Great Scottish & Western Rly
Garnet	North Yorkshire Moors Rly
Heron	Great Central Railway
Magpie	Carnforth depot
Opal	North Yorkshire Moors Rly
Raven	Great Scottish & Western Rly
Robin	North Yorkshire Moors Rly
Snipe	Great Scottish & Western Rly
Swift	Northampton Steam Rly
Car 333	as *Magna* at public house, Stamford
Car 335	Flying Scotsman Services
Car 337	Great Central Railway
Car 340	Avon Hotel, Christchurch
Car 346	as *Castra*, public house, Stamford
Cars 347-54	Flying Scotsman Services

Appendix One

Camping Pullmans

Between 1960 and 1963 a large number of Pullmans were converted into camping coaches, let at a rather higher rent that the already popular campers made from redundant elderly coaches. They had six bunks, a kitchen and large lounge; they were placed in pairs or singly in suitable sidings.

The Southern Region had the largest number, rising to 25; the first ones went to Corfe Castle, Sandling and Wool. They kept the Pullman livery, with either 'Holiday Coach' or 'Pullman Camping Coach' on the sides. They were numbered on the ends, P40 to P64.

The Scottish Region had 11 numbered SC40-50; there were three at Inverkip, two at North Berwick and Morar and singles at Arisaig, Corpach, Lochailort and Carnoustie. The Eastern Region also had 11, of which three were at Felixstowe Town, two each at Corton, Heacham and Hopton and singles at Oulton Broad South and Lowestoft North. They were numbered CC161-171.

The Western put out six cars, numbered W9869-74, at Marazion and Fowey. However when the use of Pullman campers had been terminated, the Western took all cars for the use of their staff for holidays at Marazion.

The Midland Region had only three cars, numbered 022260-2, placed at Bettws-y-Coed and Seascale. The latter were taken over by the Ravenglass & Eskdale Railway in 1968.

'Holiday Coach No. P41' was the former 1921 Clayton kitchen car No. 15, placed at Sandling Junction BR (S), soon after withdrawal in 1960, and scrapped on site in 1972.

Lens of Sutton

Appendix Two

Totals of Cars in use Pre-Grouping

Year	MR	GN	LCD	LBSC	LSWR	HR	SECR	CAL	GER	MET
1874	5									
1883	31	5	1	7						
1890		2		12	2	2				
1900				21	4	2				
1910				32	2		10			2
1914				36			23	10		2
1923				54			56	20	20	2

After Grouping there was considerable movement of cars between services. The total number in service in any one year is difficult to determine, however the Pullman Company began numbering its cars in 1908, taking in old cars then existing, and reached 354 by the completion of the 1960 cars.

Car No. 17 had only twenty years as *Duchess of York* before being demoted in 1915 for the new third class trains. *Lens of Sutton*

Appendix Three

Manchester and Liverpool Pullmans

The car numbers and names given to cars in 1983 were as follows:

500	Sir Richard Arkwright	548	Frances Burnett
501	Sir Charles Hallé	549	James Roule
502	Sir Joseph Whitworth	550	Ernest Rutherford
503	John Owens	551	Lawrence Stephen Lowry
504	Robert Owen	552	Ford Maddox Brown
505	Francis Egerton	553	Sir John Barbirolli
540	James Fraser	581	Sir Humphrey Chetham
543	Sir William Fairbairn	582	Daniel Adamson
544	Emmeline Pankhurst	583	Peter Mark Roget
545	John Dalton	584	Charles Scott
546	Elizabeth Gaskell	586	John Rylands

Names and numbers given in 1985 were as follows:

Liverpool Pullman

11073	William Ewart Gladstone
11074	Thomas Brassey
11076	John Lennon
11083	Kitty Wilkinson
11084	William Roscoe
11088	Sir John Brunner
11089	George Stubbs

Manchester Pullman

11077	Sir Richard Arkwright
11078	John Owens
11079	Francis Egerton
11081	Elizabeth Gaskell
11082	James Joule
11085	Sir John Barbirolli
11086	John Dalton
11087	Sir William Fairbairn
11091	Sir Stanley Matthews
11092	Ernest Rutherford
11903	L S Lowry
11904	Arnold Bennett

Nos. 11075/80/90 were designated Pullman but not named.

1991 renamings by Manchester Executive:

504	White Rose	550	Golden Arrow
506	Red Rose	551	Caledonian
548	Elizabethan	552	Southern Belle
549	Prince Rupert	553	King Arthur
		586	Talisman

(For Lakeland Pullman names see Chapter Eight.)

Appendix Four

Table of All-Pullman Trains

(Some did include ordinary stock at times but were mainly Pullman)

Names	Railway	First ran	Ceased
Birmingham Pullman	BR	12th Sept., 1960	3rd March, 1967
Bournemouth Belle	SR/BR	5th July, 1931	9th July, 1967†
Bristol Pullman	BR	12th Sept., 1960	4th May, 1973
Bradford Pullman	BR	1st June, 1974	became mixed stock
Brighton Belle	SR/BR	1st Jan., 1933	30th April, 1972§
Brighton Pullman Limited	LBSC	5th Dec., 1881	7th Nov., 1908#
Clacton Belle (Sundays)*	GER	16th July, 1922	June 1929
Continental Express	SECR	17th Nov., 1924	became Golden Arrow
Devon Belle	SR	20th June, 1947	September 1954
Eastbourne Pullman	BR	1948 Suns	irregular to 1957
Eastern Belle	LNER	3rd June, 1929	irregular, summer only
Golden Arrow	SR/BR	25th May, 1929	30th April, 1972†
Harrogate Pullman	LNER	9th July, 1923	became Queen of Scots
Hull Pullman	BR	6th March, 1967	became mixed stock
Kentish Belle	BR	31st May, 1948	14th Sept., 1958
Leeds & Bradford Pullman	LNER	21st Sept., 1925	became West Riding Pullman
Liverpool Pullman	BR	18th April, 1966	5th May, 1975
Liverpool Pullman	BR	May 1984	became ordinary stock
Manchester Pullman	BR	18th April, 1966	10th May, 1985
Midland Pullman	BR	4th July, 1960	16th April, 1966
Master Cutler	BR	15th Sept., 1958	4th Oct., 1968
Oxford Pullman	BR	6th March, 1967	2nd May, 1969
Queen of Scots	LNER	9th July, 1928	12th Jan., 1963¶
Sheffield Pullman	LNER	2nd June, 1924	Sept. 1925
South Wales Pullman	BR	27th June, 1955	4th May, 1973
Southern Belle	LBSCR	8th Nov., 1908	became Brighton Belle
Tees-Tyne Pullman	BR	27th July, 1948	30th April, 1976
Thanet Belle¢	BR	31st May, 1948	Sept. 1951
Torquay Pullman	GWR	8th July, 1929	Sept. 1930
West Riding Pullman	LNER	1927	1937, LNER stock
White Rose	BR	13th June, 1964	4th March, 1967
Yorkshire Pullman	LNER	1935	5th April, 1978

Notes:
*   Various other Sunday Pullmans have run: Sunday Pullman Express to Brighton, 1898, Sunday Harrogate 1926, Sunday Thanet 1921; seasonal and irregular.
\#   Name altered at various times; no all-Pullman train to Brighton from 1887 to 2nd Oct., 1898.
†   Suspended Aug. 1939-7th Oct., 1946
§   Suspended Aug. 1939-24th April, 1946
¶   Suspended Aug. 1939-5th July, 1948
¢   Kentish Belle from 18th June, 1951

Bibliography

Pullman & Perfection by F. Burtt and W. Beckerlegge (Ian Allan, 1948) gives a brief survey of the history of Pullmans, a list of all extant cars and of cars by that time out of service.

Pullman by Julian Morel (David & Charles 1983) is written by a former officer of the Company and is very good on organisation and personnel, with less detail on the trains, but does have a complete list of the 1960 'schedule' numbers, and of preserved cars.

History of Trains de Luxe by George Behrend (Transport Publishing Co., 1977) is mostly about wagons-lits activities on the Continent, but the list of world-wide Pullman cars covers the UK in detail as regards rebuildings etc.

The American Pullman Cars of the Midland Railway (Ian Allan), by J.B. Radford; a much more detailed account than is given here.

Pullman: Travelling in Style by Brian Haresnape (Ian Allan 1987); good on different body styles.

There have also been useful articles in the magazines, especially 'Pullman Postscript' by Charles Long in *Railway World*, January 1988.

Much information has also been published by Mr Terry Bly of the Pullman Society, keeping track of cars and even bodies over the years.

Class '73' No. 73 101 *Brighton Evening Argus* on the '150' shuttle in Brighton station on 22nd September, 1991, when an Open Day was held at Lovers Walk.   *P.G. Barnes*